THE CITY LIBRARY
SPRINGFIELD, (MA) CITY LIBRARY

THE
EXPERIMENTAL
LIBRARY

ALA Editions purchases fund advocacy, awareness, and accreditation programs for library professionals worldwide.

THE EXPERIMENTAL LIBRARY

A Guide to Taking Risks, Failing Forward, and Creating Change

Cathryn M. Copper

CHICAGO / 2024

Cathryn M. Copper works at the intersection of libraries, architecture, and technology. As the head of the Eberhard Zeidler Library at the University of Toronto, her current research explores technology and experimentation in libraries. She has spoken on the topic of experimentation at several national and international conferences including the Association of College and Research Libraries and SXSW EDU. Her talk on the use of artificial intelligence and augmented reality in libraries was featured as one of the "biggest and most pressing ideas" at SXSW EDU.

© 2024 by Cathryn M. Copper

Extensive effort has gone into ensuring the reliability of the information in this book; however, the publisher makes no warranty, express or implied, with respect to the material contained herein.

ISBN: 978-0-8389-3965-9 (paper)

Library of Congress Control Number: 2023033898

Cover design by Kimberly Hudgins.
Book design and composition by Karen Sheets Design, Inc. in the Lorimer and Merlo Tx typefaces.

⊚ This paper meets the requirements of ANSI/NISO Z39.48-1992 (Permanence of Paper).
Printed in the United States of America

28 27 26 25 24   5 4 3 2 1

For my most important experiments,
Leonard and Otis.

CONTENTS

Introduction *ix*

Part I A Culture of Experimentation
1. The Power of Curiosity *3*
2. What Makes an Experiment? *13*
3. Everything Is an Experiment *25*

Part II The IDEEA Anti-Method
4. IDEATE *41*
5. DESIGN *57*
6. EXPERIMENT *71*
7. ENGAGE *85*
8. ASSESS *101*

Part III Mapping Experimentation to Your Organization
9. Fail Forward *119*
10. Reskilling the Information Professional *129*
11. The Experimentation Roadmap *143*

Bibliography *159*
Index *163*

INTRODUCTION

How do technology companies innovate so rapidly? What infuses start-ups with the ability to take big risks? These are the questions I sought to answer when writing this book. Many of the changes libraries have responded to over the last two decades were born from technology companies and innovative start-ups. Understanding what fuels these sectors could help information professionals respond better to change. Libraries have, to a notable extent, responded to the technological and societal changes of the twenty-first century. Still, as someone who started studying the profession in the early 2000s, I have spent much of that time in response mode. Thus, I wondered if experimentation could be the tool that could move librarianship from a reactive to a proactive profession. Serendipitously, as my research unfolded, experimentation grew even more prevalent as a method used by innovative companies to test and launch new products, and I started to explore the idea of adapting this concept in libraries.

The beauty of experimentation is that anyone can do it regardless of budget. You do not need to be a computer scientist to conduct an experiment, which is fantastic because I am not one. The thread throughout my career has been working with and learning from architects and designers. As an architecture librarian, most of my experience comes from the academic realm, at institutions that vary dramatically in scale and scope. I started my career as a professional librarian at a small, private teaching institution in Southern California. Beyond offering a daily dose of vitamin D, the region was a haven for young, aspirational twenty-somethings. Many of my peers embarked on careers with technology giants or quit steady jobs to launch the next great start-up. Around the same time, mobile technology was taking off, and I began experimenting with how architecture education could utilize this new technology. Inspired by my peers' ability to take risks, my interest in new technologies, and my work at an institution that offered flexibility and autonomy, a foundation for approaching librarianship as an experiment incubator was born.

More recently, my experience landed me at leading public research universities with a bigger budget but less autonomy. Having worked with no budget and with big budgets, with limited freedom and endless freedom, and under traditional leadership and progressive leadership, I can confidently say that experimentation is possible anywhere. Experimentation is about more than lucrative funding and fancy technology. It is about taking an iterative approach to trying new things. What I have learned from supporting the design disciplines over the years is the value of a process of opening yourself up to wild ideas, having those ideas critiqued (sometimes harshly), adapting your ideas based on feedback, and then doing it all over again until you have something ready to present to the world. As explained in *The Experience Book: For Designers, Thinkers & Makers*, "The 'designed experience' is not a product, at least not in the finished sense. It is an ever-evolving platform for collective action(s)."[1] Therefore, in the same way architects think about their designs and the built environment, which are constantly in flux based on how people perceive them and use them, experiments offer libraries opportunities to adapt too—by trying ideas, gathering input, and making informed decisions.

This book is intended for an audience beyond librarians. Any mildly risk-averse sectors can benefit from experimentation. Although many come from academia, examples of experimentation highlighted in the book are drawn from public and school libraries and non-library government sectors. There is no limit to who can implement experiments or at what level of an organization somebody can introduce them. Some chapters speak directly to the role of leadership and management in creating cultures of experimentation. In contrast, other chapters encourage a grassroots approach to experimentation, to emphasize that there is no single "right way" to experiment.

This book is organized into three iterative parts, each of which offers insight into an aspect of experimentation. Although not everything in each part must be implemented to create an organization that experiments, elements from each of the three parts are required in an organization that genuinely experiments. Trying, tweaking, and trying again the ideas presented in this book will help you decide what aspects of experimentation work best for you.

The book's first part focuses on creating cultures of experimentation, a core aspect of organizations that take risks and innovate. Looking at experimentation through the lens of technology companies and start-ups, it dives into the characteristics of these two sectors and disentangles the techniques that make them experimentative. Chapter 1 explains the importance of incorporating curiosity into work and daily life and speaks to how technology companies and start-ups encourage curiosity. Chapters 2 and 3 then examine what an experiment is, why it is necessary, and how it can become a part of everything you do.

Building on these ideas, the book's second part presents a method to take what we have learned from technology companies and start-ups and implement it in libraries. The process known as IDEEA—ideate, design, experiment, engage, assess—walks through five areas that you can develop when starting to experiment. (I actually consider IDEEA to be an anti-method because no "method" for experimentation could theoretically exist.) Chapter 4 discusses design thinking, which plays a leading role in the brainstorming or ideation phase. Once you identify a testable idea, prototyping allows for some experimentation with a minimal upfront commitment. The prototyping phase may have many or only a few iterations, but ultimately one (or all) of them will help solve the problem you are seeking to answer. Chapters 5 and 6 focus on the concept of prototyping by breaking it down into designing and experimenting. An experiment is only complete once you engage users in testing and identify the pros and cons of a prototype. Then you can decide how and when to move forward based on this data. Chapters 7 and 8, respectively, discuss these last steps—engagement and assessment.

The book's final part is about bringing the culture and method of experimentation to your organization. Chapter 9 speaks directly to the importance of failure because no culture that encourages experimentation can exist without failure. The nature of experiments means there will be many failures, so the book presents thoughts on embracing and learning from them. Chapter 10 highlights the skills needed to experiment. Because information professionals already possess most of these, the focus of the chapter is on how to leverage those skills and create teams that thrive on experimentation. Finally, chapter 11 presents a roadmap to bring experimentation to your organization. It offers multiple paths to build a library that embraces risks and tries new things.

At the time I was writing this introduction, generative artificial intelligence became a buzz phrase in libraries. Everybody is eager to figure out what role libraries will play in using, developing, and teaching this new technology. I wonder whether this is also an experiment. I read an article in *TechCrunch* that described the brilliance of OpenAI's ChatGPT, an artificial intelligence (AI) text-generating tool, like this:

> The short explanation is that tech moves fast and big companies move slow, and while Google released paper after paper and tried to figure out how to fit AI into its existing business strategies, OpenAI has focused on making the best models and let people figure out their own applications.[2]

In this case, the laissez-faire approach of the underdog won. Instead of aiming for a finished product, which was the approach of some of the tech giants, OpenAI's style was to create a prototype, launch it, and see how it developed—a true experiment. Like OpenAI, we too are living in the age of experimentation and trying to figure it out as we go along. If you are willing to take the risk, you will likely reap the reward.

This book is not a how-to book but rather a toolbox of ideas that you can choose to implement. The tools in this book will help shift your approach to projects to one that is flexible and adaptable and will increase your appetite for risk-taking and experimentation. By doing experiments, you can acquire the skills needed for experimentation and innovation, so take what works for you and jump in.

Notes

1. Adam Scott and Dave Waddell, *The Experience Book: For Designers, Thinkers & Makers* (London: Black Dog Press, 2022).
2. Devin Coldewey, "Google Takes on ChatGPT with Bard and Shows Off AI in Search," *TechCrunch*, February 6, 2023, https://techcrunch.com/2023/02/06/google-takes-on-chatgpt-with-bard-and-shows-off-ai-in-search.

PART I
A CULTURE OF EXPERIMENTATION

chapter 1

The Power of Curiosity

At its inception, the iPhone was a series of experiments that eventually transformed our everyday lives. Arguably the most innovative product in history, the iPhone was Apple's answer to combining an MP3 player with a phone, the solution to a problem it anticipated after the release of the iPod, its handheld digital music device. Apple identified that the need to carry two separate devices would frustrate consumers, and it sought to beat its competitors by developing a device that combined a phone and a music device. Fortuitously, executives were already experimenting with multitouch technology. The first application of the multitouch technology was a table-sized prototype. Once this prototype was greenlit, more followed, and eventually, through a series of experiments, the first iPhone was born. Today Apple has a reputation for leading innovation in the technology sector and changing how we use technology. Innovation, at any level, is vital in all industries to move ideas forward and improve upon existing concepts. Using the technology industry and start-ups as models for how libraries can use experimentation to innovate, we can discover concrete ways to incorporate experimentation into our everyday work.

Whether you, as a user, are aware of it or not, technology companies are conducting experiments on you all the time. The type of experimentation and openness to trying new things that Apple exhibited in developing the iPhone is commonplace in the technology industry these days yet underutilized in other sectors. This culture of experimentation has the potential to revolutionize slower moving disciplines like librarianship. Although librarianship is full of habits and expectations that engender a reluctance to change, such as a dependence on data and statistics, we can reframe these same ways of working to encourage more experimentation and innovation in library environments. For example, the need to use statistics to inform decision-making, which sometimes prevents librarians from trying new ideas, is a critical component of experimentation. Instead of using low numbers as a definition of defeat, librarians can use those numbers to test prototypes, pilot projects, and make decisions about retooling an initiative or sunsetting long-standing programs to introduce new projects. Likewise, you can use experiments with high use to support a case for a full-scale operation and increased funding (concepts which I will discuss in more detail later in this book). While experiments can often be unpredictable, they have the power to make library work more efficient and forward-thinking.

Any existing hesitation in libraries does not mean that librarians are not trying new things. Many are, and this book highlights some of them. But realistically, there are hurdles to experimentation in libraries, likely stemming from the routine need to defend budgets and maintain usage statistics. These real feelings of fear, uncertainty, and doubt that circulate in the library profession lower the threshold for rejection. Yet a relatively simple shift in culture and thinking can lead to an influx of innovation. Simply framing new initiatives as experiments and testing them as prototypes gives you more liberty to take risks and fail; therefore, the likelihood of innovation increases. Experiments are a tool to keep up with the rapidly changing landscape in which libraries operate. New or existing initiatives can be constructed in an explorative fashion, thus providing librarians with a tool to investigate new concepts before making serious commitments. Experiments can quickly adjudicate what does and does not work and provide solid data to decide what changes you want to implement in your library. To be clear, not all experiments lead to breakthroughs. In fact, very few do. Most experiments result in incremental improvements to existing initiatives. However, investing in both breakthrough and incremental paths to innovation is worth the time and energy.

The Difference between Creativity and Innovation

To achieve those breakthroughs or incremental improvements, we need to start by talking about how creativity and innovation fuel experimentation. Contrary to what many believe, you do not have to be creative to innovate. You must be curious, but everyone can be curious. Curiosity means you want to learn more or try something new, a critical soft skill for people in the technology industry. Because technology moves so fast, those who work in the industry need to be passionate about growing and adapting. This same mindset is essential for librarianship. Even though the profession does not always move quickly, it is constantly changing. Curiosity blossoms when you identify a gap in your knowledge. This does not have to be a grandiose concept but can be as straightforward as wanting to know more about digital resources in a specific subject area or how to bring awareness to an event series held in your library. Whatever you want to learn more about, get curious about it and start looking for ways to experiment.

Technology companies rely heavily on creativity. Creativity allows your mind to conceive new ideas and act on them, an outgrowth of curiosity. In other words, curiosity is searching for new ideas, and creativity is realizing those new ideas. Experiments are a tool that can help move you from curiosity to creativity. When you unleash the potential to discover new ideas through curiosity, aha moments are inevitable. Use your curiosity to look outside your immediate areas of interest for possibilities to expand your knowledge and creativity. Participating in conferences at the intersection of technology and information or attending lectures about a subject outside your expertise are among the avenues to widen your thinking. When you expose yourself to other environments and changes happening in other industries, you give yourself the freedom to make new connections with people or ideas outside your discipline.

Innovation comes from taking risks, and experiments provide an incremental approach to risk-taking. The other parts of the equation, curiosity and creativity, help you achieve innovation. As shown in figure 1.1, creativity enables you to develop an idea, and innovation is the work that makes it viable. Simply put, you will not be innovative unless you are curious and creative, and doing so usually means breaking away from the status quo.

Within the technology sector, there is a growing acknowledgment that innovation is the centerpiece of strategic development and launching new initiatives. We can translate the same mindset to the information profession. Technology companies invest in understanding their markets and developing cutting-edge products. They do this by observing real people and situations and testing ideas with prototypes and experimentation. With little additional effort, libraries can make this a priority too. Librarians know a great deal about their users, and by borrowing techniques from other industries, such as design thinking and experimentation, we can expand our knowledge and use that understanding to inform decisions.

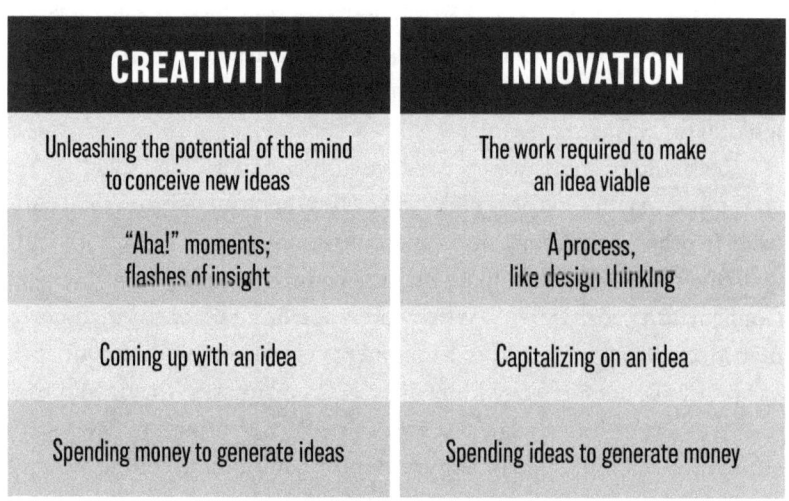

FIGURE 1.1 Enhancing Innovation

After all, you can improve any idea. Technology companies understand this concept exceptionally well. Apple never stops improving the iPhone. Imagine trading in your phone for an earlier model. It would feel ancient, even though it may only be a model or two older. Like Apple, libraries seek to improve continuously. The status quo can change as quickly as the newest iPhone model by testing and implementing new ideas through experimentation if it becomes a routine process for libraries.

A Culture of Experimentation

At its core, experimentation is about a willingness to try new ideas or introduce changes to existing initiatives. Start-ups, in particular, do this exceptionally well. They are the epitome of experimentation. They operate in highly uncertain environments. They probe for new possibilities and look to the future. Every start-up takes a risk, tests a new idea, and tries to scale up its business model. Therefore, every start-up is an experiment. Even though most start-ups face uncertainty and a high risk of failure, the no-fear approach to "winging it" gifts them the potential for substantial success. There is a high percentage of failure in start-ups, but those who fail often find great success. This is because they are focused on what is not yet being done. The most successful start-ups are the ones that build something entirely new and make it essential.

An example of such a success is Dropbox. Today most people are familiar with Dropbox as a leading file-hosting service. However, it started as a pilot project launched by two MIT graduates in 2007 that developed into one of the most valuable start-ups in the world. Its core purpose, like experiments, was to solve a problem. Its founder, Drew Houston, conceived the idea when he repeatedly forgot his USB drive. To address the issue, Houston started with the most straightforward product possible, a cloud-based platform to save and share files. He did not try to do too much, and he did not try to do too little. This barebones concept gave the infant company a prime opportunity to test and improve the product quickly. The prototype-like model bypassed the traditional development model that involves long incubation periods. Instead, he launched the product with the minimum number of features needed for viability and then asked for feedback. During the feedback-gathering phase, Houston discovered that a hurdle for users was understanding how to use the file-sharing product. Dropbox deployed quick how-to videos in response, and the start-up took off. This experimental approach enabled Dropbox executives to seek feedback early and take simple steps to improve the product.

Start-ups and technology companies spark new ideas and encourage off-center thinking. Many have accomplished this by creating cultures of experimentation that permeate all levels of their organizations. These organizations understand that the most innovative ideas emerge when the entire ecosystem experiments, so they put a premium on innovation and creativity. This model of experimentation works because it gives everyone in the organization a platform to continually try out new technologies and designs without the fear of failure.

Of course, these companies have an advantage that libraries often do not. They usually have hundreds of thousands or even millions of users, which makes experiments more feasible. They can quickly test a new website feature with a subset of fifty thousand users without affecting the bottom line or disturbing daily operations. This vast audience also means they receive important feedback with minimal effort. Yet experimentation is only possible with a pragmatic interest in innovation. Although most libraries cannot have ten thousand people test a new service, they can still benefit from being more curious and creative. Librarians are good at using data to get results. Their data-collection and analysis expertise, coupled with an increased appetite for innovation, is an ideal equation for more library experimentation. The pool of people available to test ideas may be smaller, and the experiments' impact may not change how we live our everyday lives. Still, the bones of experimentation have enormous potential to increase library creativity and innovation.

Experimentation has transformed industries like technology and entrepreneurship. Today almost all technology companies incorporate experiments into their research and design, and the boom in start-up culture paved the way for increased risk tolerance. Using experiments, organizations have a tangible tool to obtain a clearer picture of the value their product or service brings to the consumer. You can use the knowledge gained from experiments to make a pitch for continuing to invest in a product or service, developing it on a larger scale, or adapting it into a new idea. Experiments can help entrepreneurs, employees, and executives refine ideas and put them into practice where they want to see change. Organizations that embrace experimentation can account for specific goals, push boundaries, and innovate within their fields.

The low bar of entry for experiments makes them a highly useful tool to fuel innovation. Libraries can successfully borrow ideas and build on the experiment revolution that the technology and start-up industries have started. Like these industries, initially, all that is required is to be curious and want to learn more about a topic or initiative. Then the experimentation process often starts with design thinking and low-cost data collection. Most libraries have already built data collection into their intellectual infrastructure. You can use that data and your curiosity to power new initiatives. To formulate experiments, discuss problems with users or try design-thinking exercises with your team to explore new ideas. Once you have a picture of what you want to explore, you can begin the experiment. Running pilot projects or prototypes to see how people might respond to a new idea allows you to get feedback early and revise as needed. Libraries with multiple locations may be able to experiment with an idea in one space before launching it across all library locations, a viable way to scale experimentation to libraries. A simple approach lets you test ideas and challenge practices that dominate the field.

Launching experimentation in libraries is not a technical concept. Instead, it is a cultural concept. Access to funding and technology is not what makes a good experiment. Applying your curiosity to what you know about your organization will encourage you to test meaningful new ideas. The mechanisms of experiments are less important than creating a culture in which experimentation can thrive. Creating a culture where people feel free to experiment with experimentation is critical. Imagination and passion are the enablers of innovation. By nature, most librarians are curious people who want to learn more. After all, the core contribution of the information profession is being a part of the learning and exploration process. Libraries can build on this characteristic by following the lead of technology companies and start-ups that have excelled in creating cultures that take risks and learn from failures. Transparency and communication around experimentation are vital to creating this culture. Companies that tell the story of their experiments, even if an experiment fails, are the ones that truly boast cultures of experimentation.

So, what can we learn from leading technology companies and experimental start-ups? An organization that encourages curiosity and exploring ideas through experimentation will, in the end, become more innovative. This book discusses how to map those practices to your library organization, but you can start now by using a few simple techniques. First, start asking "why not?" instead of "why?" "Why not?" expresses an optimistic outlook that will motivate you to try something even if it might fail, because curiosity does not thrive in cynicism. This mentality will help you and your colleagues be more curious and open to taking risks.

Next, stay close to the action. If you are curious about what innovative companies are doing and what practices they are adapting, be sure you take the time to learn about them through reading or networking. Gatherings like South by Southwest (SXSW) provide an unparalleled opportunity to peek at the latest and upcoming trends in technology. Staying in the know regarding new technologies and the shifting user base prepares you to respond to library changes and increases your motivation to do so.

Another practice frequently seen in technology companies and start-ups is an office environment that fosters play and discovery, where thinking and acting like a kid at work is encouraged. When you take time to disengage from your routine activities, you allow your brain to make connections that it might not have before. Google famously has playground slides in many of its office locations, which sends a message to its employees that having fun is part of the work experience. As a practice, model the behavior you want to see in your organization and from senior management. You might not have control over an entire organization or department (or the resources to install a slide in your library), but taking steps to be more open to possibilities helps build curiosity and creativity in your everyday work. You are on the road to experimentation if you can incorporate curiosity and discovery into your daily work.

The Experiment Revolution

We are still very much in the early days of an experiment revolution. Technology companies and start-ups have proven what is possible with experimentation. The practice will continue to evolve, and more industries will build it into their routines to keep pace with innovation. Accelerating technologies like augmented reality and artificial intelligence requires a massive experimentation capacity. Libraries have just begun to explore these technologies. To keep pace with developments in other sectors, an increased capacity for risk-taking is necessary. Thankfully, libraries do not need to completely reinvent themselves. Many libraries are already engaged in experiment-like activities, but reframing them as experiments will inspire creativity across the discipline and pivots libraries to a more innovative mindset. Libraries that are infused with a culture of experimentation will be the ones that have breakthroughs and transform the discipline. They will be the ones with the big ideas. Embracing the power of curiosity and exploring ideas through experimentation positions libraries to adapt to the future.

chapter 2

What Makes an Experiment?

To a degree, experimentation already exists in libraries. Many information professionals test new ideas, gather data, and adapt existing services, which raises the obvious question of why a cultural shift is even needed. If libraries are already doing this, then why put in additional time and effort? A structure for experimentation within an organization will increase innovation and deliver a message that the organization is willing to try new things. Because many libraries are already testing new ideas, a shift to embedding experimentation firmly into library cultures will lead to a higher tolerance for risk and a more remarkable advancement of innovative ideas. Innovation is simply a good idea executed well, and experimentation is a trusted method for executing good ideas.

Because the technology sector was an early adapter of experimentation, it can be viewed as the ultimate test bed for proving its benefits. The culture of experimentation in the technology sector was driven by the low cost of experimentation. Thanks to technological advances, experiments no longer require expansive new infrastructures. Instead, incremental changes, like tweaking an existing webpage's layout, can yield the desired data and results. Libraries can adapt what the technology sector has demonstrated—that small changes can make big differences.

Technology companies figured out that experiments do not necessarily require new resources or time commitments. You can often test new ideas with the resources you already have available. All libraries desire more staff and funding to implement new ideas, but experimentation can be the answer to those challenges. One of the most cost-effective things an organization can do is to test ideas before committing to a large-scale effort. If investing in a prototyping lab for your library involves renovating a space and hiring additional full-time employees, first test the concept by installing a few 3D printers in an underutilized space in the library. This low-cost experiment can build the case for the prototyping lab, but even if the full-scale lab never comes to fruition, you will have accomplished something. If we hold out for the FTE or renovated space, we miss the opportunity to try something new. Even though experimentation may cost money upfront yet not show an immediate return on investment, the long-term benefits of spending a small amount can get you to where you want to be in the long run. The point is that small-scale experiments that require little time and effort can create an enormous impact on resources, services, and employee morale. Experiments are the starting point for new initiatives and improvements. Once you have proven a concept, making the argument for long-term investment is easier.

Prototyping in Experiments

People often conflate prototyping with experimentation. Prototyping is a product of experimentation, but it is not the entire process. Prototyping is a rough model or draft version that helps you disprove or validate a hypothesis. You are looking for an outcome when using prototyping as a problem-solving method. For example, in architecture school, one of the first skills students learn is to build models. Concepts like scale, material properties, and structural systems are critical to architecture education, and students learn these through model-making. Yet the more important purpose of model-making is to test designs. By taking designs from 2D to 3D, models help designers identify the stability of the structure, how daylight will illuminate the space, analyze its form, and so on. Models serve as a prototype for the actual building because they allow architects to solve problems early in the design process and are thus an essential part of that process.

Trying concepts out on a small scale will help you identify problems or areas for improvement before making a total investment. The theory behind prototyping is simple—it is better to realize the building won't stand at the point you've only made a plywood model rather than when you are in the full-scale building process. Similarly, prototyping lets you act before you have all the answers. As a decision-making process, most people find it is easier to have something to critique than just throwing out ideas to see if they will stick. By starting with a rough concept, if you stumble or the prototype fails, you will have the chance to recorrect as you go.

Prototypes are a way of asking and answering questions. Although they may result in more questions than answers—a desirable outcome in the early stages of experimentation—all prototypes yield answers by helping you to understand what does or does not work. Sometimes the most obvious solution will be the best. On the other hand, if your hypothesis is invalid, you will still have made a discovery. Either of those two outcomes will be valuable because promising prototypes do not just communicate findings. They persuade in decision-making. You can use the data and results of well-tested prototypes to decide on next steps.

The Origins of Experimentation

Understanding how the technology industry has utilized prototyping and capitalized on a rich history of experimentation will help you understand how experimentation looks different in various disciplines. In libraries, experiments do not necessarily fit the more recognizable mold of scientific experiments.

The twentieth century's revolution in computer and information technology opened new doors for companies at the cusp of innovation to embrace experimentation. However, although most disciplines use a model of experimentation that mirrors the scientific method, technology companies have reinvented experimentation types to fit their needs. Some technology companies, like Google, conduct more than ten thousand experiments annually. This quantity-focused approach to experimentation relies on a type of experiment known as the A/B test. This method uses randomized experiments with two variants, allowing the company to test two different product versions to see the customer's reaction. For example, a hotel booking company may have the current website version with a yellow "Book Now" button and another experimental version with a blue "Book Now" button. If the company determines that the blue button gets more people to complete bookings, it will likely decide to change it to blue permanently. This simple method of experimentation allows companies to make many quick decisions that increase their profit margins.

Finding the correct type of experiment that meets the needs of the discipline or project is critical to successful experimentation. Depending on industry-specific needs, experiments look and feel different. In general, there are three types of experiments.

Experiments that happen more organically than others are known as natural experiments. Experiments in this group can be as simple as predicting an outcome and then observing what actually occurs. These do not require controlling any variables. In libraries, a natural experiment might be watching how users use a new piece of technology and for how long. Making observations in the natural library environment may help inform future decisions on the need for technology and other equipment in the library.

On the more controlled side, many disciplines operate within a lab experiment model. This means that the elements of the experiment are controlled, yet they can certainly happen outside a lab setting. The A/B tests referenced above are lab experiments because there are two variables, one is controlled, and one is uncontrolled. In many medical experiments, patients are divided into three groups: one will receive a high dose of a new drug, a second will receive a low dose, and a third group will receive a placebo (i.e., the independent variable). In this way, lab experiments allow for more control and influence. Lab experiments are less common in libraries but not nonexistent. For example, if you are interested in improving your library website, consider conducting A/B tests or trying different versions of the website to gather feedback on what works best.

Finally, field experiments could be a natural or lab experiment that takes place in a real-world setting. Most library experiments are field experiments because they are conducted in a user's natural environment, which is usually the case when libraries test their resources and services. Examples of a field experiment in a library could be testing new furniture designs or layouts. Later, I will talk specifically about doing space experiments in libraries, as there are many ways to experiment with library spaces, be they big or small. Using the library as your "field," you can try a new chair design, sleep pod, or soundproof booth, for instance, by starting with an existing one or a prototype and collecting data on how it is used and its value in the library experience. Note that all industries do not utilize field experiments. Different disciplines have different incentives and capacities for experimentation, so a one-size-fits-all solution is impossible. As you read this book, think about what makes sense for your organization and what aspects of the examples and suggestions are worth adopting.

Whatever type of experiment you conduct, stay aware of the possibility of bias and stick to data-based decision-making. Experts have written extensively about the different types of research bias. Research bias occurs when research is heavily opinionated or single-sided, makes unsupported claims, or leans toward a certain outcome. These implications threaten to skew the results of experiments. Other types of bias run the same risk. For example, status quo bias refers to what occurs when people prefer that things stay the same, an obvious obstacle that needs to be addressed and can be through experimentation. Intuition bias lends itself to people who always want to trust their gut instincts. Using experiments to respond to these types of bias can help to identify the best solution more clearly. However, more severe forms of bias exist, such as implicit bias. This term describes unconscious attitudes toward people or stereotypes of particular groups. Make yourself aware of implicit bias towards certain groups when conducting experiments. A test developed by Harvard University, the Implicit Association Test (IAT), can help identify any potential implicit biases and ensure future experiments are neutral.[1]

Do All Experiments Need to Be Scientific?

Experimentation provides a systematic approach to designing, evaluating, and making decisions. You can frame projects of any size and budget as experiments. An experiment could be as simple as introducing a portable 3D printer or as complex as creating a new department in the library that offers a wide range of data services.

Experiments are heuristic tools that aid in making important discoveries. In libraries, experiments are not necessarily scientific, though they may include some elements of the scientific method. Scientific experiments usually include control groups, treatment groups, independent variables, and dependent variables. Factors such as these are crucial when testing pharmaceuticals on human subjects, but can be far too stringent for library experiments. Most library work is not scientific, so you do not need to hold experiments to a rigorous standard. Instead, library experiments borrow elements from the scientific method, such as a hypothesis and testable variables. For most library experiments, the control group is the status quo, and the dependent variable is the thing you are testing. Therefore, it is wise to do some benchmarking before you get started. If the control group is the status quo, it is essential to have metrics to compare the status quo to the dependent variable. For creating a new department to support data services, consulting statistics on existing services and usage is prudent. Before starting a new department, you should know the number of requests for data services, how many people are utilizing the services, and your expenditures. In this case, benchmarking existing metrics is critical to the success of the experiment.

However, a truly innovative idea may not have a status quo to compare against benchmarking data. When you cannot benchmark an initiative, it is especially critical to test it as a series of experiments. This way, the experiments are iterative and can build on the metrics of prior investigations. For example, simply launching a data services department would not be the place to begin if the library wants to offer data services but has yet to gain experience in this area. Instead, research and prototype the idea first. Adjust the job responsibilities of one person for a trial period so they could offer a workshop on data management and individual consultations. The trial period provides some initial data and helps inform the next steps. If the experiment meets the objectives, you could extend the trial period, and another person could offer a data visualization workshop, and so on.

Experimentation across Sectors Today

Thanks to the ongoing evolution of the digital world, technology companies run experiments constantly. They can find out what customers want by testing a product before launching it on a large scale. A poster child for experimentation, Amazon founder Jeff Bezos directly attributes the company's success to the number of experiments it conducts. He believes that "success at Amazon is a function of how many experiments we do per year, per month, per week, per day." Leaders of many technology companies understand that cultures of experimentation spawn innovative ideas, so they have made experimentation a core aspect of their businesses. Intriguingly, these companies do not run a few experiments. They run thousands of them. Bezos explained that the low cost of experiments means Amazon can test more ideas: "If you can increase the number of experiments you try from a hundred to a thousand, you dramatically increase the number of innovations you produce."[2] To adapt this approach, libraries must build experimentation into their DNA. When experimentation is limited to one department within the library, there is no organization-wide culture of experimentation, and the innovation potential is limited. Technology companies with an authentic culture of experimentation facilitate prototyping and testing for everyone in the organization. Like Amazon, increasing the number of experiments conducted will result in more innovations, so embedding it throughout the organization diversifies the areas that are testing ideas, leading to a richer pool of innovations.

In technology companies and start-ups, experimentation is a vital part of the research process that leads to innovation. These companies make a substantial annual investment in research and design (R&D), but this investment has yet to become common in the service sector. Historically, the service sector undervalues R&D, even though the existence of such organizations is dependent on its users. All libraries, especially public libraries, provide a service to users. These services compare to technology company products, so where technology companies use experiments to test products, libraries can use them to test services, their equivalent of a product. So why has the service industry yet to adopt research and design to the degree of the technology sector?

Technology companies and start-ups are dependent on a steady stream of new ideas, whereas libraries often hold onto legacy resources and services, even when these no longer serve users well. The perceived need to hold on to existing initiatives may arise because some library organizations lack structures to bring new ideas forward. In addition, as already discussed, libraries, in general, are risk-averse cultures. Drawing from technology companies, making a small upfront investment in understanding user needs and testing concepts will help library decision-makers determine what services and initiatives to pursue by arming them with data and eliminating fear and riskiness. Like the scientific method, experimentation tests a hypothesis and collects data to prove its veracity. It is an iterative process, where one experiment informs the next. Libraries that commit to R&D that includes experimentation will deliver better services, adapt faster, and add more user value.

The success of libraries depends on users using their resources and services. Libraries can use research and design to develop new or improved resources and services. The library's resources and services, along with its staff and space, create an experience for the library user. Like companies constantly seeking to improve their products, libraries can implement systems to improve their services and experiences. To accomplish this, leaders need to nurture curiosity, data needs to be valued, and workers need to conduct experiments. These aspects must be translated from the technology sector to create cultures of experimentation in the service sector. Technology companies and start-ups show that employees thrive when they can be creative and curious. Further, the emphasis on R&D and data-based decision-making prove that when it comes to making good business decisions, data outperforms intuition. Encouraging library professionals to experiment is the answer to increasing R&D and data-based decisions in libraries. Finally, a cultural shift is needed to map experimentation from the technology sector to the service sector. A greater focus on R&D across library organizations empowers everyone, not just those whose job responsibilities include user experience or assessment, to investigate areas for growth.

In libraries, we talk a great deal about resources and services, but the library is as much an experience as anything else. Try to imagine an exhilarating library experience. Perhaps upon entering the library, the first thing you see are gigantic, bright neon words on a wall behind an open service area that say "Experiment. Play. Try something new." As you walk into the library, a digital touch screen invites you to browse a list of current library experiments. Some experiments are easily identified as such, like a tabletop robot to practice coding and a tablet with digital storytelling tools displayed on a technology bar near the front of the library. Others, like a new gallery wall displaying a collaborative art project or the Thomas Heatherwick-designed Spun Chair, appear less like experiments. Further into the library, you notice a glass walled-off area labeled "Tinkering Lab." Unlike other library maker spaces, library workers in the lab are playing and prototyping alongside library users. Some people are exploring crafting materials, while others are testing generative AI. As you move through the library space, you notice that print and digital media are intertwined. In the stacks are touch screens to browse digital library content alongside the analog media. Upon leaving the library, a touch screen asks you to rate the experiments you encountered. These subtle features in the library space communicate that library leadership is open to experimenting, and that a library is where you can experience new things.

A satisfying library experience will keep users coming back, which ultimately leads to library impact. Yet what keeps users coming back is constantly evolving. Libraries can use R&D and experimentation to try out new ideas and improve the library experience continuously. Experimentation that includes prototyping, data, and a human-centered approach are critical to creating a visionary library that provides a cutting-edge experience. In the scenario above, part of the experience comes from users providing feedback on the experiments, so that they can help decide which direction the library goes.

What Else Is Missing from Libraries?

In addition to a lack of user research and focus on the experience, there are other reasons libraries fail to innovate. Too often, a change in strategic direction does not result in robust changes. Organizations that are cautious, such as libraries, usually focus on predictable, short-term results. The comfortable route for most libraries is to take the small win. Instead of making sweeping changes, if a tweak to an existing initiative checks the box for the strategic direction, then that becomes the preferred option due to its low-cost, low-risk appeal. For example, a library could develop a digital literacy framework and host workshops on such topics to meet the strategic goal of expanding a digital literacy program in an academic library. These efforts meet the goal of developing a digital literacy program. Yet taking minor actions like these discourages innovative activities. Alternatively, an experimental approach that asks library employees to explore new and exciting avenues has the tremendous potential to inspire creativity. Empowering people to test digital literacy course content, collaborate with faculty on course development, or look beyond digital literacy to visual and artificial intelligence literacies may require a more uncertain, long-term commitment. Although the less predictable outcomes of these initiatives may cause uncertainty for leadership, these activities push the boundaries of what it means to expand a digital literacy program, and pushing the boundaries is how you innovate. Experimentation carves an incremental path to more impactful initiatives.

In libraries, limited time and budgets have created cultures where employees feel restricted and resist trying new things. The typical library culture rewards resource utilization and process standardization. It is focused on fulfilling existing user needs instead of anticipating unspoken needs. In other words, library leaders are comfortable using monetary resources efficiently and effectively, not with spending on pilot projects or fact-finding initiatives. This budget and operational management style creates a repetitive and predictable work environment. Most library employees spend their time on day-to-day operations and repetitive tasks. Even academic librarians, who seemingly have more freedom to investigate research interests, find themselves in a predictable annual cycle. The repetitive nature of library work has unintended consequences for innovation. In companies that reward innovation, job requirements constantly change and there are few routine tasks. Leading technology companies offer project-based work, so as soon as a team completes one project, it is on to the next, which may have different outcomes and mean working with a completely different set of people.

Although a complete overhaul of library work would be a fascinating experiment, I will make more concrete suggestions in this book. Designing internal structures and processes that promote sharing ideas and prototyping can empower professionals and organizations. Surprisingly, you can accomplish this with minimal effort and without any new resources. Little changes go a long way. At the core, all that is required is a shift in mindset to want to try new ideas. Once you try new ideas, you can determine whether it is a positive change, making implementing long-term innovations less uncertain.

Not only do experiments provide data for decision-making, but they also lead to more creativity and innovation in multiple capacities. Organizations that experiment cultivate a growth mindset. Structured and intentional experimentation tells library employees and users that the organization is enthusiastic about trying new things. Communicating a strong message indicates that leaders are committed to a culture of risk-taking and a willingness to fail. In return, leadership is rewarded with fresh ideas and an engaged community of workers. For more creativity and innovation to come out of an organization, senior administrators and middle managers must embrace experimentation and the uncertainty that comes along with it because the culture of the organization is established and executed at these levels. (Part III of the book will discuss the role of management and how and why their support is needed to make experiments work.)

When done well, experiments result in small-scale changes, which are the first steps in making impactful, long-lasting change. Because experiments operate as a series of micro changes, there is a higher tolerance for risk and significant return on investment. Even in change-resistant organizations like libraries, evolutionary change is possible through small investments, keeping you ahead of the status quo and anticipating the future. At first, experiments may feel like they are high-risk, but in contrast, they are a low-risk solution to tweak existing initiatives or test new ideas. Experiments are test beds that require a minimal budget, time, and energy investments. The return on investment is that people start thinking in new ways, concepts move forward, and all levels of the organization are empowered.

An experiment is about the process, not the result. Borrowing from the scientific method and design prototyping, experimentation gives libraries a mechanism to test ideas, get feedback, and make incremental changes. As you will learn in the next chapter, opportunities for experimentation are everywhere. Think about your dream library. What does the experience look like? Now start using experiments to pilot minor aspects of the bigger picture. The visionary library discussed early in this chapter only manifests in stages. Through various experiments and iterations libraries can be constantly evolving. That in itself is an experiment.

Notes

1. Harvard University, "Project Implicit," https://implicit.harvard.edu/implicit.
2. Jeff Dyer and Hal Gregersen, "The Secret to Unleashing Genius," *Forbes*, August 14, 2013, www.forbes.com/sites/innovatorsdna/2013/08/14/the-secret-to-unleashing-genius/?sh=635c9836361c.

chapter 3

Everything Is an Experiment

Experimentation is built into the DNA of start-ups and is evident in their core values. To cut through the noise in an oversaturated technology and product market, start-ups operate as labs for experimentation. Because their outputs must be unique, they constantly test new ideas or ways to improve existing products. Libraries can be experimentation labs too. You can view every resource, service, renovation, or any other aspect of the library experience as an experiment. Doing so situates libraries as agile organizations, able to pivot and adapt quickly in rapidly changing environments.

There are obvious differences in the scale of libraries compared to technology or start-up companies. Generally, libraries have smaller audiences and are not motivated by profits. This difference puts libraries in a unique position to experiment for the social good, benefiting the most significant number of people in the largest possible way. Library experiments can enrich users' lives in forms other sectors cannot. When motivated by profits, companies often take a self-serving approach to experiments, with the bottom line operating as the primary decision maker. On the other hand, libraries can align themselves with experiments that genuinely make a difference in the library user's experience, regardless of their potentially smaller user base. By constantly seeking to improve the user experience, everything you do becomes an experiment.

The only thing needed to turn a library into an experimentation lab is a simple shift in mindset. Experimentation, at its core, is nothing more than a cultural shift in how we approach problems. Although it may seem that experiments must test the newest, most expensive technology, that is far from the truth. Organizations with cultures of experimentation understand that making incremental improvements to existing products is an essential part of experimentation, if not more so than implementing the latest technology. Even approaching daily tasks as experiments can improve organizational efficiency.

My team conducted an experiment to test new methods for file saving. There were apparent inefficiencies in saving files to our in-house server, such as the inability to collaboratively edit the same edition of a file and difficulty accessing them from offsite. As the leader, I framed the process as an experiment. For one month, we would try saving specific files to a cloud-based server, and then collectively we would decide what was better for our workflow. It took little time to see the benefits of sharing and saving files in the cloud. The trick was to frame it as an experiment, which helped move the team in the same direction. Even the most resistant employees do not see it as an end-all, be-all commitment when it is an experiment. Instead, it allows everyone to test-drive a solution and provide feedback before making a decision.

To make this cultural shift, experiment as frequently and widely as possible. As mentioned above, approaching an everyday task this way becomes an exercise in thinking experimentally. It is important to emphasize this insight to your team, department, and organization because ultimately experimentation is not just the responsibility of one person but that of the organization. To implement a genuine cultural shift, you must offer everyone in the organization the opportunity to experiment in one way or another. You can begin by experimenting with what is in your purview and then showcase the impact of those experiments to others.

Changing an organization's culture can be ignited at any level. Chapter 10 discusses in more detail the role of administrators and managers in creating a culture of experimentation, but for now, you can change the way you think and approach problems with the knowledge that a cultural shift is not an individual who thinks experimentally; it is an organization that thinks experimentally.

Think of all the projects on your to-do list that never go beyond the piece of paper, likely due to an already overstretched workload. Taking an incremental approach that allows you to test one aspect of the project can make them more obtainable. Further, this experimental approach helps you build the case for testing future iterations and securing needed support. Your to-do list should not consist of fully developed ideas. Instead, think of pilot projects. Taking a more impromptu approach is sometimes necessary when pushing the boundaries and testing ideas.

One of the libraries I led had a collection of about five hundred physical architectural drawings. Although the use of the drawings was consistent, digitizing the collection would increase their accessibility and help preserve the physical copies. Digitizing the collection was a top-priority project until we lost a full-time staff position to the main library on campus. Instead of taking it off the to-do list, I encouraged the rest of the team to move forward with the project but reframed it as a pilot. Instead of committing to a monstrous project to digitize all five hundred drawings, we would digitize the fifty drawings that were best suited for digital access. If we could figure out a way to do more once the pilot was completed, that would be a bonus. On the flip side, if we could not manage to digitize all fifty, that would be informative too. Taking this low-risk approach helped the team fit the task of digitization into their workflows. More significantly, I used the impact of those fifty drawings, which was measured by increased use and reach, to make a case for additional digitization support. One example of the impact was demonstrated when an international researcher discovered one of the digitized drawings and included a facsimile in an exhibition. Ultimately, we adapted workflows and developed a new digital collection for accessing the drawings. Rather than feeling as though they were conducting a cumbersome experiment, team members were able to learn a new skill set and align the project with our strategic goals.

Experiments that test a library initiative or idea primarily fall into three categories: technology, program, or space. I consider the example of digitizing architectural drawings a technology experiment since it tested digitization workflow and technology. An example of a programming experiment that I have worked on is an event series. After graduate school, I was hired as the first professional librarian hired at a small academic library. To activate the library, I decided to test an event series that engaged the campus community and situated the library as a partner in the curriculum. Again, by framing this as an experiment, the level of commitment was low, and if needed I could easily shift my energy in a different direction. Yet the event series was well received, attracting a large audience of students, faculty, and community members. It became part of my annual workflow and, after the initial year, required less of my attention. The success of the initial two events created momentum, and soon colleagues recommended panel ideas and speakers to me. Like the technology experiment, the event series may have never made it off my to-do list had I not considered it an experiment.

The Open Science & Data Collaborations at Carnegie Mellon University

Another example of a program experiment is the Open Science & Data Collaborations (OSDC) initiative at Carnegie Mellon University (CMU). The OSDC provides services and a platform to make open data for research and researchers more accessible through digital tools, training, collaboration opportunities, and expert consultations.[1] In an interview with the author in October 2021, Brian Mathews, associate dean for innovation and interdisciplinarity at CMU, discussed the innovative and transformational nature of the program. In his role, Mathews develops roadmaps to implement such projects. He explained that the project is not just an experiment but also a cultural shift to get the university community and researchers to understand better and value the importance of open science and data collaborations. To accomplish this goal, Mathews guided colleagues to identify the necessary components of the project. They looked closely at the problem to ascertain why it was a problem and identify the target audience and other stakeholders. The team used this information to tailor the OSDC initiative to the right people and solicited their feedback before moving on to a larger group of constituents. From there, they would know whom to get involved and have an idea of how to proceed. They mapped the project's inputs, activities, and outputs, and initial, intermediate, and long-term outcomes. Mathews explained that laying out these project components early on helped distill it down and pitch the project to the necessary parties. Thinking about how to assess the OSDC initiative would begin later; at the onset, the focus was on launching enough of the project as a pilot to identify the gaps, experiment, and bring about a cultural shift.

This project operates as an experiment by being flexible and pushing new boundaries. The project outline is interactive, meaning that if stakeholders change or new outcomes arise, the project can pivot as necessary. A living document like this maps essential components and important milestones but is nimble and easily modified. Coupled with flexibility, the OSDC is testing new ways to facilitate collaboration across disciplines. Although most libraries have become advocates of open access and open data initiatives, CMU is taking it one step further to experiment with different ways of connecting researchers. One way it is doing this is through the dataCoLAB. This OSDC initiative brings together fields that are not connected so that data producers and data scientists with different technical and disciplinary backgrounds can work in the same space. The lab has a broad reach, inviting participants from across the CMU community and the city of Pittsburgh. In addition, the role of information professionals at the CMU Libraries is to offer support on data management, project documentation, and other research methodologies.[2] Each collaboration teaches the dataCoLAB something and offers the opportunity to implement improvements. The flexible approach, desire to change the research landscape, and continuously evolving and improving nature of the OSDC and dataCoLAB make them experiments.

The Library East Commons at the Georgia Tech Library

When I asked Mathews about the most innovative thing he has ever seen in libraries, he said unequivocally the Library East Commons (LEC) space at the Georgia Tech Library. Around 2006 the library began this space experiment by playing with ways to create different moods and ambiances depending on how library users needed to use the space at any given time. The adaptable atmosphere utilized music, colored lights, and movable furniture to create a personalized library experience. At the time, the idea was innovative because no other library was thinking about versatile common spaces, although today the concept is more familiar to libraries.

The Georgia Tech Library initiated a movement to make libraries adaptable spaces that promote well-being. The big idea was not about the furniture and the fixtures but the philosophy. Georgia Tech was experimenting with how users could alter or shape their environment for whatever they needed it to be. As a result, the library became a place that nourished users—understanding the "why" of what it was creating was critical for pushing the boundaries of the LEC. The why became the objective: to create a space where people could grow their imaginations and intellectual curiosity. This why was accomplished by experimenting with the elements within the space.

Before the renovation, the Library East Commons was a dusty reference floor with a large footprint of books. In *An Experiment in Modern Knowledge Spaces: The Library East Commons*, people describe the area as desolate and underused.[3] Leaders elicited ideas, held focus groups, and observed how people used the library to determine space preferences. Further, they explored other study and workspaces on campus to better understand why users frequented these spaces instead of the library. They sought to consider it less like a library and, with open eyes, see what was working outside the library so that they could incorporate those aspects into their design. An overwhelming trend that emerged from the research was that people wanted the ability to shape the space for a particular moment of learning or relaxation. The responses demanded flexible dwelling space, a novel concept that became a metaphor. The LEC space would be a refreshment for the body and mind.

The design was a nine-square grid, like a tic-tac-toe board. Each space was connected and continuous yet had its own defining characteristics and purposes. The design tested the juxtaposition of individual and collaborative spaces. The renovated LEC boasted modular infrastructure with walls that could move to create different size spaces and levels of privacy. The Georgia Tech Library experimented with the space's elements and how the LEC would function. At the heart of the LEC was an art and performance space that experimented with offering free pizza, karaoke nights, and speed dating. By trying these types of unusual events, the library was testing to determine the ideal balance between study and socializing. And yes, students who wanted to use the library as a study space found it distracting, but the experiments facilitated finding a balance (figure 3.1).

FIGURE 3.1 Library East Commons / PHOTOS BY BRIAN MATHEWS, 2008

As opposed to a more traditional approach to library design that caters to solitary scholars, the LEC was an adaptable environment that sought to experiment with how people would use it—gradually implementing changes to the sociological, architectural, and intellectual use of the space allowed for feedback along the way. The modular walls, lighting, and everything in between were part of the experiment, but what makes this experiment stand out from others is that it was just as much testing a philosophy or a way of thinking. The independent and dependent variables of the experiment were the users and the space. It was testing how they could affect each other.

The LEC renovation sought to prove a concept. As a prototype, it was intentionally gritty and slightly unfinished. Mathews says it was his favorite project and the most innovative thing he has seen because "it was like going from playing clean guitar to distorted guitar. It was edgy and radical for its time, and we were figuring it out as it unfolded." There were small interventions and different iterations, but eventually, the lessons learned from the space experiment informed a complete renovation of the library and a sizable addition. Today, the Georgia Tech Library is sleek and modern.[4] This new iteration builds upon concepts from the LEC prototype, which was ultimately about changing the way users think of and use libraries. Everything in the LEC was an experiment. It transformed knowledge spaces and rewrote the library experience. Instead of merely being a way to manage library spaces, the LEC helped reframe libraries as learning environments and elevate their reputation and role on campus.

Web Design at Wayne State University Libraries

An incremental and iterative approach has been pivotal in moving technology experiments forward at Wayne State University (WSU) Libraries. In an interview with me in January 2022, Elliot Polak, the assistant dean for discovery and innovation, shared that library innovation involves constantly trying new things and a willingness to keep learning about the organization, environment, and services the library offers. Polak has successfully led innovation at WSU Libraries by making small changes over time. His team always has a vision or long-term goal and implements iterative design and continuous improvements to achieve that goal.

The article "Start with an Hour a Week: Enhancing Usability at Wayne State University Libraries" presents an example of this approach.[5] In 2016, the discovery and innovation web team redesigned the main library homepage to create an intuitive interface to access information, resources, and services. The site launched unfinished, but the team wanted feedback from real users, so they used user-centered testing modeled from Jeff Gothelf as described in, *Lean UX: Applying Lean Principles to Improve User Experience*.[6] The model utilizes a guerrilla-style method to retrieve continuous feedback, a fan-favorite in the technology and start-up worlds. WSU Libraries used a user-centered path to redesign their website by hosting hour-long usability tests each week for two semesters. An advantage to this method over a more traditional focus-group approach is that it requires no budget or preparation. The authors explain that this approach "can be successful with minimal planning, minimal staffing, minimal equipment, and minimal time."[7]

The experiment tested minor changes to the website that added up over time. As detailed in the article, each week, for one hour, members of the web team would set up a table with computers in a central library location. They recruited participants on the fly to spend five or ten minutes responding to a series of scripted tasks. This informal method provided the web team with immediate feedback that they could implement before the next week's testing and was notably the most productive hour of their week. The iterative approach was the most crucial part of the experiment. Regular user testing allowed the team to make small changes built on each other rather than abruptly overhauling the entire website, which could run the risk of disorienting users.

Of equal importance, the success of the website redesign project led to an increase in user-focused improvements beyond the library homepage. A minor change that had big results was rephrasing the "Ask a Librarian" feature, a chat service for users to communicate with research experts in the library. User testing showed that changing the location of the Ask a Librarian feature and information on how to use it could reduce confusion and be more in line with an intuitive interface. Changing the branding and location of the legacy link was not without resistance, but ultimately within a month of making these changes, the chat service increased by 70 percent and showed people across the library that small changes can have a significant impact.

Other changes to the website were not without their roadblocks. Any experiment, especially those that seek to change a legacy service, may face some resistance. In our interview, Polak said he lets resistance guide his team because it almost always leads to opportunities to build better services. When someone opposes a change, the web team responds to that feedback. In the case of migrating to a new discovery interface, opposition inspired an innovative solution to the problem. Responding to concerns about how the new interface ranked the relevancy of physical materials held in the library, the web team experimented with integrating the metadata from the discovery interface into a custom, in-house design that separates results by item type and utilizes an artificial intelligent plugin by Yenwo. The web developers could then show the impact of the change and shift people's mindset about experimentation. Polak said their goal is to accommodate all use cases and needs with a user-focused approach. As he explained, "Library discovery tools should always be looking forward for ways to improve the experience for all people at all levels of the organization. By working through incremental change, we acknowledge that our current solution is not perfect, but we are working toward that perfect solution over time."

Polak attributes the innovation and forward-thinking approach at WSU Libraries to the library leadership and its "Visionary Pillars" model.[8] Creating a positive working environment where library employees are empowered to try new things is one of the four focus areas for WSU Libraries. It reinforces the importance of creating a culture around experimentation in libraries. To establish this culture, WSU Libraries hosted an optional Leadership Academy for all library employees. In the interview, Polak said it was the most innovative thing he had seen from any library. The academy was held over two semesters and offered a pathway for library workers to develop their professional, leadership, and management skills. Polak shared that it was a success because it allowed people to reach their goals and showed a genuine investment in library employee success. In return, as demonstrated by the innovative work accomplished by the web services team, library employees feel like they can try new things and push the boundaries at WSU Libraries.

Intentional versus Incidental Experiments

In all these examples, the experiments are not entirely new projects, but iterations of work that people are already doing. In most cases, potential experiments are viable projects that are already on your radar or that you are currently working on. You can simply reframe existing projects as experiments. Michael Luca, associate professor at the Harvard Business School, coined the term "incidental experiments" in the book *The Power of Experiments: Decision Making in a Data-Driven World*.[9] Incidental experiments refer to experiments you are doing but might not be aware of. Information professionals are prominent incidental experimenters. We are always developing new resources, offering novel services, reconfiguring library spaces, and testing new technologies. The catch is we have yet to frame these projects as experiments. We constantly experiment without even knowing it, demonstrating the need to shift our mentality and start thinking of everything we do as an experiment. Once you are in experimentation mode, you will notice experiments everywhere.

Experimentation is a method for systematically trying new things. Yet when everything becomes an experiment, you will notice that some experiments are intentional, and others are incidental. Both are relevant and valuable. This book primarily discusses deliberate experiments or those that are consciously planned and assessed. However, once you start experimenting, you may find that, incidentally, you have already been conducting experiments. In a previous library, I launched an "Experimentation Station," a space where we would intentionally conduct experiments. With this infrastructure in place, I soon realized that everything I was doing was an experiment, whether at the Experimentation Station or not.

Before planning and conducting actual experiments, I gathered feedback on what changes users would generally like to see in the library. I collected responses by putting a poster in the library that said, "I Wish the Library had…" and letting people write ideas on Post-its and sticking them on the poster. A popular request was for more quiet, private study spaces. Instinctively I rearranged a few tables in the library to utilize nooks and corners outside the main library spaces and traffic areas. At the time, I did not think of this as an experiment, but once I was in that mindset, I realized it could operate as one. We collected data on how frequently users occupied these seating areas to support a proposal for a mini-renovation of the library space to include more intentional private seating. Incidental experiments like this helped me appreciate the value of small changes. Although I would have loved a complete renovation from the get-go, testing different seating arrangements and collecting data would make for a better renovation in the long run. Incremental improvements like these are an essential source of innovation.

The Why, How, and What of Experiments

Understanding why experiments matter helps shift your mind to think of everything as an experiment. Libraries can adapt experimentation into everyday workflows and projects. But why is experimentation the best approach to these projects? Experiments are a method to test theories or hypotheses. To learn about the all the ways users use a service, space, or resource, experiments can be an effortless mechanism to understand why and how.

From the onset, each of the experiments shared in this chapter had a goal. Knowing what you want to achieve with a task or project gives you the ability to measure its success. Wayne State University Libraries wanted to design a more intuitive library home page. By measuring the increase in use for the chat reference service, they could determine that the home page was more intuitive. The key was having a goal to achieve and something to measure. Without that, testing would only tell you what people are doing, but not why they are doing it or how they are doing it. Although understanding what users are doing with library resources, services, and space holds value, the why and how are arguably the more important factors and where libraries have the most potential for impact.

We already know that experiments provide a framework for instituting and vetting new ideas. They serve this purpose well because they can be used for fact-finding when no precedent exists, or when precedent does exist, for finding how to adapt or retool an existing product or service to perform better. Thinking of everything as an experiment is an enlightening experience and helps you see the limitless possibilities in libraries. Take a walk around your library and identify what resources or spaces could use rehab, or observe users in action and see where they struggle. Then think about why these areas need improvement and how you could accomplish it. That's it. You have an experiment. It is that simple. Then, once you have thought about what you want to experiment with, start small and inexpensive. Use prototyping and pilots that require minimal funding to test your idea so that you can gather data and feedback to make an informed decision before launching your idea as a fully fledged resource or service. With this approach, you have the tools and information necessary to pitch any proposed change to the administration when you want to transition it from an experiment to something long-term and fully operational.

To be clear, thinking of everything as an experiment is about opening your eyes to new possibilities and breaking down barriers that may keep you from trying new things. However, not all decisions need to be the result of an experiment. You must make some decisions more immediately, and others involve more factors than just the data you can collect from experiments. Use experiments to investigate testable solutions. In libraries, these are decisions that can be measured by usage, usability, impact, or qualitative feedback. It is also important to realize that any data collected in an experiment depends on context. If something works in one context, it does not necessarily mean it will work in another. The examples shared in this chapter or later in this book might not fit your library. They may need to be adapted to align with your goals or fall outside the realm of anything you would do. Experimentation is about finding what works best to meet your professional and organizational goals.

Lean into the Grittiness

When everything becomes an experiment, whether intentional or incidental, every experiment will not be well thought out, but the point is they do not need to be. The process of experimentation is intentionally gritty. It combines passion and perseverance to reach a goal, and there is a delicate balance between experimentation and efficiency. By nature, experiments are a risk, but you must learn to be okay with grittiness. Experimentation is about allowing yourself to be comfortable with this risk for the sake of trying something new. When you try something new, you put yourself on the line. Remember that big strategic projects fail too, but at a much higher cost, so however you look at it, experimentation is worth the risk and investment. In the end, library cultures willing to take risks and build experimentation into their DNA will see more large-scale, long-term innovation and reap their rewards.

Executives at Apple took a risk when they sought to develop the iPhone. It could have been a colossal failure, but through prototyping and testing different iterations, they introduced a beautifully designed device that has enjoyed continuing success. The ongoing success is, in part, a result of their ongoing experimentation. Even Apple leans into the grittiness. I read a rumor that Apple is currently experimenting with foldable iPhone prototypes. The idea might never make the cut due to concerns over the foldability of touch screen displays and the market for foldable smartphones, yet the resistance does not stop Apple from being curious and learning more about it. Welcoming this perspective into your work will put you on the path to experimentation.

Notes

1. Carnegie Mellon University Libraries, "Open Science & Data Collaborations," www.library.cmu.edu/services/open-science.
2. Carnegie Mellon University Libraries, "Data Collaborations Lab," https://cmu-lib.github.io/data-colab.
3. Crit Stuart et al., "An Experiment in Modern Knowledge Spaces: The Library East Commons," video produced by Hugh Crawford's English 1102 class (Georgia Institute of Technology), 2006, hdl.handle.net/1853/13665.
4. Jason Wright, "Georgia Tech Library Opens in Refurbished Crosland Tower," *Georgia Tech News Center*, January 11, 2019, https://news.gatech.edu/news/2019/01/11/georgia-tech-library-opens-refurbished-crosland-tower.
5. Maria Nuccilli, Elliot Polak, and Alex Binno, "Start with an Hour a Week: Enhancing Usability at Wayne State University Libraries," *Weave: Journal of Library User Experience* 1, no. 8 (2018), https://doi.org/10.3998/weave.12535642.0001.803.
6. Jeff Gothelf, *Lean UX: Applying Lean Principles to Improve User Experience*, edited by Josh Seiden (Sebastopol, CA: Josh O'Reilly Media, 2013).
7. "Start with an Hour."
8. Wayne State University Library System, "Library System Visionary Pillars," https://library.wayne.edu/info/about/visionary-pillars.
9. M. Luca and M. H. Bazerman, *The Power of Experiments: Decision Making in a Data-Driven World* (Cambridge: MIT Press, 2020).

PART II
THE IDEEA ANTI-METHOD

chapter 4

IDEATE

Experimentation is not a fixed process with guaranteed results, but a mindset that takes a human-centered approach to innovation. The steps in experimentation are flexible and adaptable, much like the experiments themselves. Thus, insisting there is a "method" for experiments feels counterintuitive. The next part of the book outlines five essential components of experiments in libraries. Adjusting them to your organization's or individual initiatives' specific needs is encouraged. Therefore, I describe the steps below as an "anti-method" because they do not need to be entirely understood or meticulously prescribed. The term anti-method emphasizes that you try to circumvent a usual methodology or methodologies in general. When you experiment, follow the natural evolution of the experiment. Take the ideas from this part of the book that meet your needs and adapt them as necessary. Regardless of what experimentation looks like at your organization, the most important thing is that you are doing it.

The first component of experimentation is ideation, or coming up with an idea to test with an experiment. You can think of ideation as brainstorming. The point of ideation is to conceive possible projects or initiatives that will move your organization in the direction you want. This chapter highlights design-thinking techniques as a tool to help you and your teammates brainstorm new ideas. After ideation, you design the experiment. What will your experiment look like? More importantly, what do you want to learn from your experiment? Determining early on what a successful experiment looks like is an integral part of the design phase. Then you conduct the actual experiment. In chapters 5 and 6, I share examples of experiments to illustrate what they can look like in libraries. A big part of these experiments, or any experiment, is implementing and testing it. Therefore, chapter 7 shares tactics for encouraging users to use the experiments. Finally, assessing your experiment to determine how well it met the metrics of success is critical for determining how and if the initiative will move forward.

These five components of the anti-method—ideate, design, experiment, encourage and assess—constitute the IDEEA approach to experimentation. Every experiment looks different, but all experiments, to some degree, include these five components. Even if you conducted the same experiment and executed these five components identically at two organizations, the results would look different. That is what makes experimentation a valuable tool to move an organization's unique strategic initiatives forward. Going off track and mixing and matching IDEEA components to suit individual needs is commendable. The anti-method is an experiment too.

Experiments Need to Solve a Problem

You can experiment with anything. However, it is best to craft experiments around strategic goals and solving legitimate problems to make them functional for your organization. Before you begin experimenting, think carefully about what questions you are trying to answer. It is essential to complete this step *before* you start designing the experiment. Although it can be part of the design-thinking process, you should already have identified your goals and potential problems. Having a problem to solve is critical to the experimentation process. Determining the problem is the most underrated part of innovation. People often think of innovation as executing a good idea, except all *really* good ideas solve problems. Think back to the iPhone example at the beginning of the book. Apple wanted to combine a phone and an MP3 player into one single device. Identifying this human-centered problem was core to the brilliance of the innovation.

Generally, the common denominator shared by great thinkers and innovative leaders is the ability to identify and solve problems. Albert Einstein once said, "If I had an hour to solve a problem, I'd spend fifty-five minutes thinking about the problem and five minutes thinking about solutions." Einstein highlights the importance of solving the right problem because the answer comes relatively easily when you ask the right question. Another way to think of the importance of solving the right problem is to understand the "why" of experimenting. We already know the "what" is the measurable aspect of the experiment, and now you know the why is the reason driving the experiment. Once you answer the why, you can figure out the what and the how. All good experiments and innovations start with why. In Simon Sinek's TED talk, "Start with Why: How Great Leaders Inspire Action," he explains that understanding the why of your organization is critical to formulating goals and attracting a user base, and the same philosophy applies to experimentation.[1]

When determining the problem you want to solve or why you are experimenting, first look at what you already know. A brief analysis of historical and current practices at your organization or discipline can help identify weak points. Talking with colleagues or users about their frustrations with library resources or services is one way to go about this. Another avenue is attending professional conferences inside and outside the information profession. Understanding what problems others are trying to solve can help you see your organization from a new perspective.

Another method for identifying problems is to start with strategic goals and work backward to identify gaps where experimentation would assist in achieving these goals. Questions beginning with "how might we . . . " are exceptional idea generators. For example, if one of the strategic goals is to implement more technology, you may ask your team, "How might we improve access to new and creative technologies?" Then let your team go wild brainstorming. Ask each team member to come up with three ideas. This design-thinking method is called rapid idea generation and is a helpful tool for generating ideas quickly.

However, although mapping experiments to strategic goals is essential, these experiments are not solely about organizational drivers. A carefully crafted problem is necessary, so stick to the strategic objectives that accommodate asking relevant questions. Sometimes issues need to be more broadly focused. If the problem identified was how to achieve a 30 percent increase of the use of e-books about Jacob Lawrence, an African American artist, it is likely too narrow. Does it matter if users want to learn more about Jacob Lawrence, or are you hoping that, in general, the diversity of artists researched increases? Also, if the goal is to see a rise in the use of diverse materials, whether this takes place in print or digital form is irrelevant. Avoid setting yourself up for failure by making the problems too specific. Think about the big outcomes you hope to achieve and concentrate on the place between the detailed outcomes outlined in the strategic plan and the outcomes you genuinely care about.

You can also find potential problems along the periphery of your daily work. These are "invisible problems." They are less evident than those that may be documented in strategic plans. If you are considering the problem of how to get diverse materials used more, be sure to consider all sides of the issue. What conditions created it, and what conditions does it make? We know that less material is published that represents diverse authors and topics. That is a condition that creates the problem of low use. In addition, for academic libraries, not having diverse content taught in the curriculum is a factor in low library use of such resources. A condition that the low use creates could be a general lack of awareness of the contributions of underrepresented groups. Look closely at these outlying issues to determine if there is a problem that you can explore through experimentation. Pay attention to details and keep an open mind.

A concept map is a helpful exercise to dig deep for core problems. Start with what you think the problem is and create branches to represent the causes and effects of the problem. Often the most interesting issues are the ones that are two or three levels of separation from the original problem. In the concept map shown in figure 4.1, the initial problem was to increase the use of equity, diversity, and inclusion library resources. As that problem is unpacked, more specific and approachable

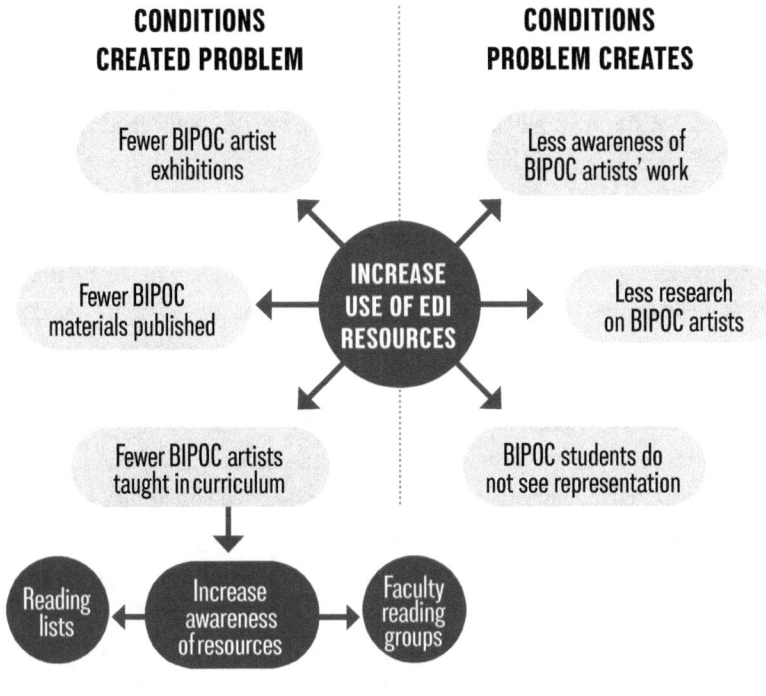

FIGURE 4.1 Concept map

issues emerge. For example, a condition that creates the initial problem is that artists who are Black, Indigenous, or people of color (BIPOC) are not featured frequently in the academic curriculum. Hence, a secondary concern is a need to increase awareness of BIPOC artists' resources to use in the classroom. Then practical experiments like hosting faculty reading groups and creating reading lists emerge.

Take a Human-Centered Approach

As mentioned above, the problem that needs to be solved is sometimes obvious. To help identify problems, start-ups and technology companies invest heavily in user research. What the organization sees as a problem and what the user sees as a problem can be completely different, yet ultimately the user is the expert on what they need. In libraries, we must listen to the users, whether community members, professionals, faculty, or students. Talk to them to find out what they feel is missing from the library experience. Involve them in the brainstorming process by asking questions, either formally or informally. Surveys and focus groups can be effective ways to get feedback from users, but so can informal chats.

Gathering feedback from users on potential improvements is critical to developing a good product or experience. To get a deeper understanding, using the library resource or service can help you see it from a user's perspective. If you are interested in improving e-book access, take the e-book platform for a test drive. You may notice roadblocks you otherwise would not have when you experience it from the users' point of view. You may need to select a filter in the discovery layer to highlight e-books, or find that choosing between reading online or downloading the item is confusing. Of course, many libraries do not have the ability to make changes to third-party e-book platforms, but creating step-by-step user guides, short instructional videos, or training staff about how to explain the process to users could all be potential solutions to the problem.

Another exercise, lifecycle mapping, is a valuable in better understanding users and their relationship to the resource, service, or experience. This tool offers another human-centered perspective by illustrating the different stages of experiencing an element of the library. In lifecycle mapping, the library user is not the end user but a part of the process. The purpose of a lifecycle map is to highlight the actions users take and the people involved in that process. Lifecycle maps require empathy and an understanding of the user. When complete, a lifecycle map shows the processes tied to the action of people and how one action can impact the progress of the entire cycle.

A lifecycle map can take two forms. For academic libraries, for example, it can map the trajectory from student to scholar and highlight the points in the curriculum where a student benefits from the library. The student lifecycle can give insight into what students are learning in the curriculum and therefore be beneficial to bridging experiments to the active learning process. You can adapt this form to reflect other types of libraries by identifying the moments or reasons a user interacts with the library. Alternatively, a more general approach is to map a library user group's purpose, outcomes, behaviors, and conditions (figure 4.2).

If I'm thinking about the architecture students who are my immediate user group, the library's purpose may be to support research in the creative design process. An outcome may be embedded library research and instruction in the architecture curriculum. To envision behaviors or how users interact with one another, I imagine the library as a lab for creative research where users are designing as they are conducting research. Finally, stakeholders like faculty and administration need to buy in to accomplish these outcomes. Making these types of connections helps unpack actual problems relevant to the user. At what points are they required to interact with the library? Who are the players involved in those experiences? Where are the weak points or potential for more involvement?

FIGURE 4.2 Lifecycle mapping

You can do the same with a library resource or service. At first, asking these questions may appear to complicate the problem development process, but on the contrary, this activity gets to the real problems that often hide below the surface level. Breaking down the user or service into component elements helps you understand the entire experience and can transform it to better resonate with users. Remember that as with the experimentation process, it is okay to have different iterations of your problem. Be flexible in developing your problem and let it evolve as you go through the research and experimentation processes.

What Is Design Thinking?

Not surprisingly, design thinking was born out of the design disciples. When a business depends on designing items for human use, taking a human-centered approach to problem-solving is critical, and that is precisely what design thinking offers. Design thinking encompasses the aspects of human-centered design that are the most learnable—insight, observation, and empathy. In traditional problem-solving, you take a linear and structural approach. For example, a new event series at the library brought a low turnout, so you might think about possible reasons this was the case. It could be that advertising was inadequate, the timing was inconvenient, the topic was not attractive to users, and so forth. Once you identify potential reasons, you think of solutions. This traditional approach to solving problems results in possible solutions but impedes innovation because it happens in isolation. In comparison, a human-centered approach to problem-solving, such as design thinking, taps into our innovative capacities.

IDEO, a leading design firm from San Francisco that now crosses the globe, has been credited with bringing design thinking to the mainstream. To inform external partners, it launched IDEO U, which at the time offered courses on design-thinking methodologies to organizations.[2] It has since expanded its reach by offering these courses online. Another example of how IDEO has led the design-thinking revolution is by developing toolkits like the *Design Thinking for Libraries Toolkit*.[3] This toolkit offers library-specific activities to understand the needs of users and engage communities. Thanks to IDEO's work through IDEO U and the toolkits, design thinking is no longer restricted to design professionals and has been adapted in nearly every sector.

The most important thing to remember is not to operate in a vacuum when utilizing design thinking. To fully benefit from this human-centered research approach, design thinking requires engaging other people, your team, and the community. One person cannot and should not make all the decisions about library spaces, resources, and services. Design thinking should include key and potential stakeholders, including library administration, support staff, and users. The ideation process is enriched by incorporating multiple perspectives and will help you achieve the goal of solving the right problems.

Fundamentally, design thinking is an explorative process that seeks to enhance discoverability. Much like the IDEEA anti-method for experimentation, there is no right way to do design thinking. Instead, you may do multiple iterations of a design-thinking exercise and get different responses each time. At its core, design thinking taps into three capacities—insight, observation, and empathy—that everyone is capable of but are often overlooked in traditional problem-solving methods. Incorporating these three elements into design thinking, as will be discussed in detail below, is to take a human-centered approach to answering problems and conducting experiments. When you deeply understand your user and are genuinely empathetic to their needs, it will result in the best product possible. Tap into your innovative potential and ask questions that you may not have proposed when using traditional problem-solving, because better questions yield better solutions.

Insight is the foundation of design thinking and also of innovation and experimentation in general. Insight is a strong understanding of people's emotions, behavior, or beliefs. This level of knowledge about the user is the key to accelerating good ideas. Insight into why the user behaves a certain way can come from design thinking, experimentation, and an analysis of historical and current practices. Both traditional and human-centered research methods provide insight into what, how, and why users prefer certain things. Overall, the trend for circulating print materials in academic libraries has declined over the last decade. The assumption is that users prefer electronic materials or can find more information on the internet. However, taking the time to understand why circulation counts were historically high and what motivates users' current practices yields additional insight. By digging deeper into this problem, we realize that not only have user preferences changed, but the research environment is also changing. The lower circulation counts are not necessarily a reflection of libraries alone, but academic research and curriculum changes more generally. Students are increasingly assigned team-based projects that require interdisciplinary work, and the days of individual essays, for better or worse, are fading. These new forms of knowledge creation and expression have led to increasing use of articles and data because the monograph does not always provide the relevant and immediate information that student research projects demand. With this insight, we know what and how students' research has evolved, but we also have a deeper understanding of why print collections are not as valued as in the past. These insights are critical to how we respond to the problem. Insight is about moving beyond assumptions to understand the motivations behind a user's behavior.

Observation, another critical element of design thinking, is an effective way to gain and build on insight. Several observation techniques allow you to learn more about user behavior and interests. Simply talking to the community about their wants is a form of observation. Focus groups can be another powerful tool for observation when you use well-chosen why questions and participants are encouraged to tell stories. Observing users undergoing ordinary tasks in the natural library setting can open our eyes to potential problems. Watch for visual clues when a library user checks out a book or searches the catalog. Is it a pleasant experience, or do they seem frustrated? What parts of the process frustrate them?

One way to think of observation is to think like a young child. Imagine you are entirely new to the world and actively learning how everything works. Children have no predetermined idea of how things should work and, as a result, find fascination in aspects of daily life that adults find mundane. To think like a child, you must ask a lot of why questions. Asking why can help reframe the problem and open the possibilities to a more innovative answer. Embrace your inner child, ask a lot of why questions, and observe users in their world to understand new perspectives. Taking this naive approach is a critical part of observation.

Watching people in their natural environment helps you better understand the problem. Simply observing how people use the library space or service is a form of design thinking. If you can truly immerse yourself in a world without preconceived notions, you open your eyes to new possibilities.

The last core component of design thinking is empathy, which is encompassed in insight and observation. Empathy is the foundation for understanding your user. Therefore, taking an empathetic approach to gather insights and observations helps you achieve empathy. Remember that design thinking stems from design, which is an inherently empathetic undertaking. Designers are designing for someone else, so to understand how the design will best meet the user's needs, designers want to understand what their users are thinking and feeling. Libraries are user-focused entities and can benefit from a mirrored human-centered approach to all their activities. When identifying the problem, take an empathetic approach to the research. Investing time and effort upfront to empathetically understand your user's needs and wants can have a substantial payoff later in the experimentation process. This reframing of your thought process allows you to develop initiatives that get at real problems because you are engaging with the user, who is the expert on their needs and most affected by the results.

Brainstorming

Now that you have an idea of the problem you might want to solve and have embraced basic design-thinking principles, it is necessary to understand the importance of brainstorming. Brainstorming is part of the ideation process, and there are techniques for brainstorming that will help you get the best results. Momentum and conversation help brainstorming sessions to be successful. Start with a creative warm-up activity to set the tone for a brainstorming session. Setting the tone is especially critical when a group of people may not know each other that well or do not brainstorm frequently. A playful exercise like the run-on stories you may have created as a kid works well for this. Write a starter sentence like, "One summer day . . . " for each small group on a piece of paper. Then give the papers to one person in each group. Instruct them to complete the sentence, fold the paper to hide what they wrote, and write a prompt for the next person. Continue this series of actions until everyone in the group has written one or two sentences. Then take time to read the stories out loud. This simple exercise prepares participants to think creatively and breaks the ice.

Next, present a well-honed problem statement. Think back to the example of declining circulation rates in academic libraries. The problem is less about the lower usage numbers and more about the changing research environment, so the problem statement might be "how might libraries respond to a changing academic research environment that values team projects and multidisciplinary approaches to problem-solving?" Notice that the problem is not about libraries but focuses on a specific user need. Problem statements focused outward on a particular user need or service enhancement yield better results. Then let the design thinkers go wild. It is crucial that everyone involved, whoever they may be—staff, users, stakeholders—knows that brainstorming is about quantity, not quality. At the beginning of a design-thinking session, clarify that brainstorming is not a time for critique or debate but rather an opportunity for people to feel comfortable sharing their most outlandish ideas. One technique to encourage a large number of ideas is to number them. Numbering ideas motivates people and helps them move between ideas quickly. Once you record an idea, immediately write the following number to encourage the next idea. This also helps later when discussing and moving between ideas rapidly.

Brainstorming works best as a slightly unstructured, visual exercise, so make Post-it notes and permanent markers available. An idea on a brightly colored Post-it visible to everyone in the group gives people something to talk about. Post-its also allow you to move ideas around quickly and group like ideas together. In the spirit of being visual, encourage participants to be visual too. Ideas can sometimes be communicated through images. Drawings and sketches trigger the creative side of our brains and provide us with a different set of tools to share ideas. Drawing as a medium to deliver a message helps us look at problems differently than common words and numbers. The idea of brainstorming is to be a bit crazy, so do not worry about being a good artist. You never know where a silly idea might lead.

Try using emerging technologies like generative AI for brainstorming. Idea generating tools can provide a starting point for discussion or fledgling ideas that you can expand on. Throw your library's vision and user-focused problem into a generator and see what it gives back to you. I trialed the idea-generating software Ideanote to spark some new ideas for our annual plan. The prompt "how might the Eberhard Zeidler Library offer premium information services for customers?" generated three useful responses:

1. Eberhard Zeidler Library could offer virtual house tours of different architectural styles, locations, and eras. These virtual house tours could include interactive elements such as 3D renderings, augmented reality, and additional information about the architecture, interior design, and history of the houses.
2. Ensure that patrons have access to digital versions of the library's physical resources, including books and other research materials. Offer access to digital resources through an easy-to-use platform with a wide range of search options. Offer interactive tutorials to help patrons navigate digital resources.
3. We can offer a premium service by creating exciting events and activities that engage our customers. Examples could include a monthly book club, workshops on digital tools, or group tours of the library. We could also host events with authors or special speakers or offer online forums for users to discuss their research and get feedback from our librarians.

Next, I plan to take these ideas back to my team to digest and discuss. Tools like these have the potential to jump-start new initiatives and are exceptional alternatives to add to the brainstorming toolkit.

Design-Thinking Exercise Examples

EXERCISE 1: How Might We . . . ?

> **Design-thinking exercises should encourage open-ended inquiry.** "How might we . . . ?" questions do just that. When you pose prompts this way, they are broad enough to encourage innovative thinking but

narrow enough to keep the team focused. Reframe the problem you are trying to solve as a "how might we . . . ?" question and write it in the middle of a whiteboard or on a piece of paper mounted to the wall. Then ask each participant to take five minutes to write at least three responses on separate Post-its and place them around the question. Giving participants a target number of responses produces a higher quantity of ideas. In addition, having time constraints requires people to write ideas down quickly. In design thinking, a set number of ideas and time limits are creative constraints. This rapid idea-generation exercise increases the number of generated ideas and pushes people to think a little bit more wildly than they might have otherwise. As a result, the responses to the "how might we . . . ?" question identify possible areas to experiment and test solutions.

EXERCISE 2: News Article

The next exercise taps into the visual part of our brains. Ask participants to imagine in five years what a news article about the experiment would say. Will it highlight how the experiment led to a significant innovation? How have libraries changed the way they engage users? Did the experiment fail and launch a completely different initiative? Then ask participants to draw an image to go with the news article, which will trigger the more creative parts of the brain. This exercise helps set outcomes for the experiment and simultaneously can ignite new experiments. Figure 4.3 is taken from a design-thinking workshop I led to brainstorm what role the library might play at a proposed innovation campus. The activity asked participants to write a leading paragraph that captures three outcomes and draw a picture to complement the article. When discussing the news articles and images, the image likely provides more clues about the message the person was trying to deliver, as confirmed by the image shown in figure 4.3. It also serves as a tool for people to express ideas they might not have the words to describe. By starting with the desired outcomes of the experiment, this exercise provides the tools to build backward to what it will look like to best align with the desired outcomes.

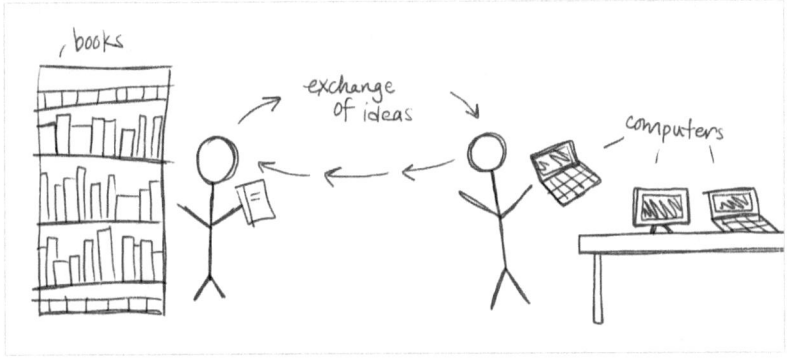

FIGURE 4.3 News article activity

EXERCISE 3: Mood Board

To continue with the visual aspect of design thinking, the third example is creating a mood board. Mood boards are ideal for library space experiments. You can create mood boards physically or digitally but opt for the physical experience when possible because it offers participants a more lively and engaging experience. If you decide to have people create mood boards on their digital devices, they should work in the same room to build off of each other's energy and be more collaborative. For a physical process, lay out magazines, posters, discarded books (preferably with lots of images), and other visual materials for participants to utilize. In the digital environment, a shared folder can be preloaded with pictures or provide a list of websites to gather images. Give participants a prompt like "create a mood board that encourages productivity in the library but is also child-friendly." Then give people twenty to thirty minutes to browse images, select the most inspiring ones, and affix them with tape or glue on a large poster board. At the end, ask participants what aspects of their mood boards could be tested and have others respond to the ideas.

Keep a record of all the ideas generated during the design-thinking exercises. Even if they do not fit your immediate need, they may be helpful later. In addition, keep a list of potential experiments to test in the future. For ideas on design-thinking exercises, check out the *Design Thinking for Libraries* website at designthinkingforlibraries.com or books like *Thinkertoys: A Handbook of Creative Thinking Techniques* and *Gamestorming: A Playbook for Innovators, Rulebreakers, and Changemakers.*[4]

How to Choose an Experiment

Once you have determined a problem and brainstormed possible solutions, it is time to choose an experiment. The rest of the chapters in this section will go into how to design and assess experiments; for now, a basic understanding of what ideas deserve an experiment will do. First and foremost, start with the experiment that likely solves the problem. If there is a clear winner, test it, but be willing to deviate from it if necessary. Further, prioritize the experiments that best align with your organization's strategic goals. Aligning with strategic directions makes it easier to present a case for a more robust initiative. Another consideration is to proceed with low-cost or low-difficulty experiments. There will likely be some budgetary constraints you must work within, so choosing experiments with the most return on investment is key. Think about whether you can effectively scale the idea. Can it be tested on a small scale and implemented later on a larger scale? Consider all these questions when choosing what experiment to try, then pick one, or two, or more. Trying lots of okay ideas can get you further than investing in one flawless idea.

Notes

1. Simon Sinek, "Start with Why: How Great Leaders Inspire Action," filmed September 16, 2009, in Seattle, TED video, 18:34, www.ted.com/talks/simon_sinek_how_great_leaders_inspire_action/c.
2. IDEO, "IDEO U." www.ideou.com.
3. Chicago Public Library and Aarhus Public Libraries, *Design Thinking for Libraries: A Toolkit for Patron-Centered Design* (IDEO, 2014), designthinkingforlibraries.com.
4. D. Gray, S. Brown, and J. Macanufo, *Gamestorming: A Playbook for Innovators, Rulebreakers, and Changemakers* (Sebastapol, CA: O'Reilly Media, 2010); M. Michalko, *Thinkertoys: A Handbook of Creative-Thinking Techniques* (Clarkson Potter/Ten Speed, 2010).

chapter 5

DESIGN

Like everything in experimentation, the way you design an experiment is meant to be flexible and adaptable. However, considering a few factors early in the process helps ensure you use your time efficiently and effectively. The design of an experiment includes a prototype, setting parameters regarding what is and is not being tested, testing a hypothesis, collecting data, and identifying biases that may skew the results.

A popular approach to designing experiments among user-experience (UX) designers is to work in small steps and on a small scale. Imagine you are launching a new event series. Initially, you may assume that the event is your experiment. However, the event encompasses many different parts, like curating the series topic, inviting speakers, getting the word out, and other logistics. To start, pick one aspect to experiment with, such as an event poster. The poster becomes the experiment, and focusing on this element alone is much more manageable. This stage of experimentation is about developing ideas into something workable. During incubation, you can test the design or layout of the poster as well as what information you should and should not include on the poster.

The prototype is the first poster, or perhaps just a sketch of a poster. Then after seeking feedback, a new iteration of the poster is created, and so on. Keep seeking user feedback on different versions until you meet the desired objectives. A poster might seem small, but it significantly contributes to the momentum surrounding the event and event attendance. As a bonus, once you know what makes an effective poster, you can reuse that research. Once you have that piece solidified, move on to another aspect of the event series. Taking an iterative approach to experimentation and tweaking each step before moving forward offers more learning opportunities and reduces the risk of failure.

Another example of designing a prototype was when I experimented with augmented reality (AR). I was curious about the technology's capacity to bridge physical and digital resources. However, my ability to code AR software is minimal at best, and third-party software options catering to libraries are limited, so I took a different approach to pilot the project. It was simple, but I tested the idea with QR codes in the stacks. As an example, the section of books on landscape architecture had a QR code linked to a LibGuide featuring digital resources. This experiment gave me data on using QR codes to bridge physical and digital resources that I could later use to pitch the idea to a programmer or third-party software developer.

The Hypothesis and Research Questions

Some may argue that the hypothesis is the most important part of experimentation. A hypothesis is a guess about the results of an experiment. Without drawing on much research, a hypothesis proposes an idea for the sake of having something to test. For example, our hypothesis in the poster example might be that an animated digital poster will get more views. We have no data to prove this is true, but it gives us an aspect of the poster design to test. The hypothesis can guide experiments toward a more user-centered approach when used in library-related experiments.

You can develop a hypothesis that frames a user-centered experiment with a theory-validate-objective formula, but feel free to deviate from this and create one that best suits your needs. Keeping library users at the forefront of the hypothesis ensures that you structure the experiment to improve library resources, services, and experiences that support the user. First, start with a theory that addresses what needs to change to encourage library users to behave differently. For instance, your theory is that to increase low event attendance, redesigning the event poster will attract users to attend future events. Then, determine what needs to occur to validate this hypothesis. Usually, this includes analyzing metrics. The hypothesis would be proven if poster views and event attendance increase in sync. Finally, tie the hypothesis to the objective to draw attention to how the experiment will be suitable for your users. Understanding the most effective means to communicate event information (objective) will benefit users because they will be more likely to attend events that raise awareness of social justice issues (motivation). Creating a user-centered hypothesis keeps experiments focused on what matters most to library users. Use the three-part hypothesis formula (theory, validation, objective) to make users the cornerstone of the experiment (figure 5.1).

To create a user-centered hypothesis, some straightforward questions can guide the design of experiments. As stated, the hypothesis is the guiding question for all experiments. What do you want to learn from the experiment? Further, be sure that it is rooted in observations and data or that you can at least gather those insights from the investigation. Once you establish the hypothesis, determine the feasibility aspects of the experiment. Address specifics like what equipment will be needed, the required sample size, who the target audience will be, how data be collected, how long will the experiment run, and so on. Questions related to the hypothesis and feasibility are the bones of the experiment.

FIGURE 5.1 User-centered hypothesis formula

At this point the testing can begin, but taking the time to address additional factors like combatting bias and avoiding skewed results better positions the experiment for long-term success. Designing experiments to solicit the desired results would negate the purpose of piloting and prototyping. The goal is unachievable if decisions are made based on assumptions or personal interests rather than on data collected during an experiment. For instance, bias usually exists in the data collection and assessment phases of experimentation. Therefore, to address potential bias, ask yourself about the measures that will be in place to oppose systemic discrimination. Answering this question helps ensure that, if others were to conduct the same experiment in the same conditions, it would yield similar results, which would demonstrate that there was no systemic bias. Another approach to combating bias is to work in a team or ask someone to review a project plan. Peer review helps ensure decisions are based on observations and results, not on assumptions, as is crucial to a good experiment.

In the Wayne State University Libraries experiment, prompts were carefully constructed to avoid leading the user toward a desired action. For example, directly asking participants to locate the 24/7 chat service would explicitly direct users to the service, whereas presenting it in a scenario would be more like a real-life situation The prompt could be "Imagine you are having trouble finding an article in a database. How would you contact someone for help?" Always remember that if you design an experiment that directs users to the answer you want from them, you will not collect valuable data. Craft experiments so that you can determine how someone naturally uses the resource or service positions the experiment for the greatest success.

Finally, strengthen the experiment further by anticipating its value and how it reinforces strategic priorities. Tying experiments to strategic priorities has been discussed previously but is worth revisiting here. If the data indicates the experiment met the objectives, consider what additional information might be needed to get buy-in for a long-term program or project. What changes in library resources or services will be made based on the results? How does the experiment support strategic priorities? Determining these factors guarantees you will gather the needed data to support future iterations and initiatives.

Start with the Simple Solution

Once you have determined a hypothesis, a simplified model of experimentation gathers valuable data while reducing investments in time and cost. When you take a simple approach to experimentation, there is little to no impact on workloads and budgets. Take, for example, the QR code experiment described earlier. Had I straightaway tested augmented reality, the time commitment would have been much more significant because of the need to work with programmers or implement third-party software. Those aspects also obviously come with a much higher cost. By simplifying the experiment to test QR codes, we could test the idea and gather valuable data without a huge upfront commitment while innovating with access to library resources. Further, this low-level commitment gave us more flexibility to manipulate the experiment based on early results.

The bare-bones prototyping approach demands minimal time and effort, which is why it is ideal for experimentation. All that is needed is to generate feedback to drive an idea forward. Prototypes are notoriously fast, rough, and cheap, so consider what is the minimum necessary to gather data on an idea. It should be a beta version of the big idea. The three types of experiments—technology, programs, and space—can all be reduced to prototype-like versions. Usually, but not always, a prototype is tangible. Accordingly, if we were testing a new website, the simplified version might translate to a mock-up menu made of Post-its or a printed poster that can be marked up. On the other end of the spectrum, space experiments might be prototyped as a virtual model since actual renovations are rarely low cost. If you are interested in new furniture, another approach would be to purchase a small amount before investing in furniture for the entire library. The purpose of prototyping is to avoid costly mistakes. A slower, incremental approach to developing an idea speeds up its implementation over time. Otherwise, you risk launching overly complex ideas too early or holding onto weak ideas for too long.

Simple experiments not only minimize impact on existing workload, but they also retrieve the most relevant information in the most condensed amount of time. When designing an experiment, consider what is the minimum time necessary to gather the information (which could be anywhere from one week to one semester). In the technology sector, it is common for experiments to run for as little as ten days. Short time frames and fast experiment cycles create excitement and collect quick results so that projects can move forward at a non-glacial pace. In prototyping, these brief interactions allow one to touch and interact with an object without having to become an expert. The point of experiments is not to spend a lot of time to make someone comfortable with a new concept. Instead, they need only to give you enough time to explore it to form an informed decision about its usefulness. You should run experiments based on the time required to collect enough robust data. Although lengthy investigations run the risk of burnout, there must be enough time to reach your user base. For academic libraries, this could be one month or an entire semester if you map the experiment to a course project. Decide on a suitable time frame for your experiment and your institution, keeping in mind that you can run concurrent experiments simultaneously.

Objectives, Data, and Other Tools

Although testing everything from QR codes to poster designs and event topics is informative, library professionals realistically do not have time to do it all. That is why setting parameters about what you are and what you are not testing helps compartmentalize each experiment. Set the parameters or objectives before you begin experimenting. A good experiment has approximately one or two objectives. The objective is a goal you want to achieve and is testable. In the case of the event poster, the objectives might be (1) to understand the most effective means to communicate event information and (2) to recognize the type of information needed and the best layout to communicate event details. These two objectives set the parameters of what to test but are flexible enough to adapt. If, as the experiment is in process, we realize that understanding how and where to distribute the information is also valuable, these objectives allow us to pivot in that direction.

Similarly, consider what you are testing your experiment against. For most experiments, the status quo will be the control group (what you are comparing the results of the experiment to), so a means to measure the difference between the status quo and the outcome is needed. For example, we might be testing the number of event attendees or the number of poster views, so the same data from a previous event could serve as the status quo. Further, keep the objective fluid. Instead of setting an objective to attract one hundred event attendees, set a goal to increase the number of attendees without specifying by how much. Avoiding absolute numbers keeps the parameters flexible. Being held accountable to an absolute value limits your flexibility and ability to adjust what you assess on the fly. Flexibility in experimentation is critical, so keep the objectives as open-ended as possible.

Information professionals are familiar with the need to collect data for assessment, and experiments are no exception. Even when building more flexibility into experiments, it is still essential to have data to inform decisions about whether an experiment was successful and to help build the case for additional funding and support later. Brainstorming to determine what success or failure might look like enables you to make an informed decision during the assessment phase. Consider what data you will collect, such as the number of event attendees, the number of poster views, or survey data that asks participants what attracts them to posters and draws them to library events. The type of data that will be relevant depends on the experiment and what you want to know.

There is usually minimal time for data collection and assessment in librarianship; therefore, many professionals find it daunting or tedious, but you don't need to overthink it. We have already discussed determining desired outcomes, so use these as the basis for data collection. The data-collection methods should give you information on the objectives. What data do you need to determine whether you achieved the desired outcomes? How will you decide based on these results? What is the measure of success? In addition, remember that experiments that were successful at other libraries might not be successful at yours. Each organization has different users, values, and strategic directions, so what works for one library might not work for every library. Results of similar experiments can differ depending on location, demographics, funding, and other factors. When establishing data-collection methods and what success will look like for your experiment, look through the lens of your library and the specific conditions. (Chapter 8 will discuss more assessment methods.)

In addition to setting objectives that fuel data collection, look to leverage the other tools that are available at your organization. Most professionals have access to some amount of people, space, and equipment. Granted, the availability of these tools varies depending on individual situations and organizations. Include your colleagues and teammates in experimentation whenever possible. Even if you are a solo librarian, consult with colleagues in other organization departments interested in experimentation. Chapters 10 and 11 examine the type of people and skills best suited for experimentation, but whether or not you have those at your disposal, approaching experiments with multiple eyes from various angles strengthens ideas and prevents errors. As discussed in the previous chapter, including others in the ideation phase can help you see ideas through a new lens or objectives you would have otherwise missed. When designing the experiment, consider how many and which should be involved. Wayne State University ran its web design experiment sessions with three people. One person recruited participants on the spot, one ran the experiment, and one observed and recorded the results. This approach helps keep the experiment running smoothly, but more importantly, allows multiple people to weigh in on the design and assessment of the experiment.

Another tool to explore is your existing library space. If there is adequate space, a dedicated "experimentation" area of the library draws attention and lends continuity to library experiments. Spaces visible to most library users are ideal, for example, near the entrance or a common area. However, establishing a dedicated space is only sometimes possible and only occasionally appropriate. Experiments can take place throughout the library or even outside the library walls. The team at Wayne State University chose a location near the main library entrance with the most traffic. They also selected the busiest time of day to reach the most library visitors. When deciding where the experiment should take place, consider whether you need access to electricity, a Wi-Fi connection, space to move around, or any other equipment or space requirements specific to the experiment. Try your best to anticipate any technical challenges before you begin the experiment to keep it flowing smoothly.

Finally, consider using branch libraries to test a subset of the population. Branch libraries provide unique opportunities to serve as incubators since they usually have more autonomy when implementing pilot projects. Early in my career, I ran a small branch library at a satellite campus about two and a half hours from the main campus. This environment allowed me to test new ideas and initiatives with minimal roadblocks. One experiment tested a roving reference service in architecture studios. The concept was to provide research support at the point of need, in this case while students were designing. Realistically a librarian at any architecture school could have tried this, but the scale of the satellite campus made it achievable and testable. In four hours, I roamed around all the studios asking each student about their project and offering research advice when warranted. Two weeks later, I followed up on their progress and attended site visits with the class. The roving reference pilot morphed into the opportunity to co-teach architecture courses and lead instruction at the main campus. Had I not tested the concept in the incubator environment, it likely would not have had the support to grow into something bigger. Identify the distributed spaces at your organization and think about how they might operate as pilot testing places.

PGH Lab

Strategies for designing experiments differ from sector to sector, so looking to those that closely resemble libraries can help us envision how to design experiments in our organizations.

Perhaps more closely aligned than start-ups, especially to public libraries and public academic institutions, is the government sector. Despite a reputation for being bureaucratic and archaic, experimentation happens in government-run organizations and offers translatable parameters for experiments in libraries. PGH Lab, based in Pittsburgh, Pennsylvania, is a city-led initiative that connects start-ups with the City of Pittsburgh (https://pittsburghpa.gov/innovation-performance/pghlab/index.html). In an interview in December 2021, Trever Stoll, a civic innovation specialist in the department of innovation and performance, told me more about PGH Lab and how it recruits and designs experiments. He explained that the initiative stemmed from a grant-funded position seeking to answer the question, "how do you bring innovation to the city?"

Launched in 2016, the first cohort hosted three start-up companies and has been growing ever since. In the initial call for experiments, PGH Lab set its objectives to tackle specific city challenges, like rectifying a sidewalk inventory to help increase ADA compliance of city sidewalks. After five cohorts, PGH Lab moved to a less static model of experimentation. Now, it asks start-ups to experiment with objectives that address more general civic challenges like engaging residents or climate change. There is also an open call to suggest a pilot project that falls outside the available categories. When designing experiments for libraries, consider either of these two models. Experiments can address specific issues like testing methods for conducting a collection analysis or more open-ended, iterative issues like improving innovation in research help services. PGH Lab operates experiments on a six-month cycle and continuously gathers feedback to make informed decisions that enhance the process. Stoll, who manages PGH Lab, alluded to each cohort being an experiment and that they each show new and different ways of improving the experimentation process. Initially, PGH Lab allocated four months for experiments, but they quickly discovered more time was needed to recruit participants, design the experiment, and do the testing. Based on that feedback, they adapted to a six-month cycle and are now looking to transition to a nine-month cycle to build in more flexibility with schedules.

In addition to having a ratified structure for experimentation, PGH Lab offers one-on-one coaching and marketing for participants. There is no financial compensation for participating start-ups, some of which may already have funding challenges, but the benefits of partnering with the city are wide-ranging. Foremost, the program connects start-ups with a "city champion," or a mentor who sees the project through from start to finish. The start-ups further elevate their services and products with the option to use the city's social media and press platforms. As PGH Lab seeks to answer the question of how to bring innovation to the city, it is as much about building community as it is about changing a culture. Through mentorship and outreach, it challenges government organizations' perceptions and can serve as a framework for other risk-averse sectors such as libraries.

Academic librarians will be familiar with the committee approval process implemented at PGH Lab. A committee approval process allows all stakeholders and leaders to review and deliberate experiment applications. The number of people contributing to the PGH Lab review process varies based on availability, but it typically ranges from twenty to thirty-five committee members. Each committee member reviews the individual applications and ranks the proposal based on specific criteria such as its overall implementation plan, the probability of unintended consequences, and its focus on diversity, equity, and inclusion. Committee members score each measure on a scale of one to five, then the overall average score is calculated. Once the scores are calculated, the committee discusses each application and invites the top applicants for an interview and to give a presentation. In the last call for applications, PGH Lab enthusiastically received thirteen proposals. How many of those the lab can support depends on the committee's review and PGH Lab's ability to secure a city champion for each accepted experiment. Stoll said that directors working for the city are always willing to partner with PGH Lab and the start-ups if departmental staffing and capacity allow. They see the benefit of mentorship and want the pilot programs to be successful. The city champions volunteer their time and help connect the start-ups to resources, people, and departments across the city. In the final chapter of this book, a committee review process for library experiments is discussed and emphasizes the importance of mentorship and connecting experimenters with potential collaborators, as seen with PGH Lab.

Each PGH Lab experiment has a deliverable at the end of the experimentation cycle. The deliverable is assessed to determine whether it helped solve a problem, although no PGH Lab experiment is considered a failure. For example, the sidewalk inventory project resulted in a digital map that tracked foot traffic. These pilot projects aim for the start-up and community to understand government processes and have a light-bulb moment. Occasionally, the department or city champion initiates a request for proposal process to continue working with the start-up post-pilot project if they find it especially valuable.

According to Stoll, the lab considers every project successful if the start-up learns something and makes connections. PGH Lab subscribes to the theory that there is no such thing as failure because you can still learn a lot from so-called failures. When designing library experiments and developing assessment plans, the intention is not that the project should be abandoned even if you do not reach your objectives. Instead, think about how you can retool it. PGH Lab experiments are assessed not solely on whether the start-up achieved the deliverable but also on what was learned and what connections were made. Part of the design of such experiments is to allow you to fail fast and move on when appropriate. The ability to let go is another reason not to make experimentation cycles too long. It's better to determine whether an idea will not work early in the experiment rather than hang on to a less-than-mediocre concept. The PGH Lab test bed model emphasizes identifying problems, training around process improvement, and developing cost savings to develop a better product. It further reiterates the importance of design experiments so that they are flexible enough to allow you to modify incrementally.

PGH Lab is not in the business of creating products—its deliverables result from a successful partnership between the start-up and a city champion. When I asked Stoll what the most innovative project to come out of PGH Lab was, he said it was not a project per se but rather the progress PGH Lab has made in breaking down silos across the city government. It has brought communities into the process of resolving city issues and fostered many collaborations. Mapping this collaborative mentality to libraries, where operating in silos is not uncommon, will increase the amount of experimentation and innovation in the information profession. Look for partners and collaborators when designing experiments. Whose expertise can you draw on to improve an experiment? PGH Lab demonstrates that innovation is not about individual work. Take the time to identify the stakeholders and make connections to move experiments forward. Establishing interdisciplinary partnerships is critical for nurturing new ideas, whether or not an experiment is the next big innovation.

Something Is Better than Nothing

The design phase of experimentation is where the idea takes shape. It is where you determine what needs to be done and then create a path to that target. It translates the ideation phase into something tangible and testable. Experimentation should lighten workloads, move ideas forward more quickly and with less bureaucracy, and not be tedious or time-consuming. When designing an experiment, keep it gritty. The experiments are meant to be partially thought-out ideas, not finished products. After years of working in shared-governance structures, I have found that having something to critique is better than having nothing. So, develop a rough prototype and then evaluate and evolve the concept. Once you have gathered some feedback, you have something to critique and get feedback on, but too often the initial hurdle of launching the new idea and having all the pieces in place prohibits us from actually doing it. That is why experiments are slightly rebellious—because you do not need all the parts in place. You can throw an idea out there and see what sticks.

The guiding principle for all experiments should be to create a better experience for library users, but how that unfolds will vary across individual libraries. Use the threefold hypothesis formula and the guiding questions outlined in this chapter to keep your experiments user-focused. Defining the theory, validity, and objective of the experiment when formulating the hypothesis frames it so that it addresses the core needs of those experiencing problems. The experiment does not have to be complex to solve a user problem. Keep experiments simple and use the prototype model to identify potential solutions. Experiments always present challenges and limitations, but I have yet to come across an experiment that is not worth pursuing all together.

chapter 6

EXPERIMENT

You know by now that being curious and open to new ideas is core to developing an experimental mindset. Once you have adopted this way of thinking, new ideas and a willingness to try new things will start to flow. However, not all ideas fit the mold of experiments. In this chapter, I address what makes a good experiment and share examples of different experiments in size, scope, and across various library types. A good experiment, as explained in chapter 4, needs to solve a problem. The definition of "a problem" is intentionally vague: it could be big or small, but the experiment should test an improvement in some way. For example, it could solve an existing user problem like how to provide more seamless access to e-books or address a lesser-known challenge like how to reach a new audience. Whatever the problem, establish what it is you are trying to solve before you begin.

Further, although experiments could test a new approach to a routine task, they should not focus on an inquiry about your day-to-day work. If you want to, build a new idea into your daily work or test a new workflow that fits into experimentation, but just assessing a routine task is not an experiment. In fact, another requirement is that experiments challenge the status quo to some degree. Not every experiment needs to be a significant innovation, and most will not change the landscape of libraries significantly. However, experiments should advance an existing condition in some meaningful way. One method to challenge the status quo is to collaborate with units outside your immediate department, or better yet, outside the library. That said, although not a requirement it is a solid recommendation to make experiments collaborative. Including new perspectives helps you see problems through a different lens, so during the ideation process, brainstorm creative solutions to test with experiments. Finally, experiments need to test a variable and be measurable, which chapter 8 discusses in more detail. Experiments work best when they are incremental, meaning you test one aspect, tweak it, and then test it again. Building on the idea of a prototype, an experiment tests a rough idea, and collecting measurable data is critical to developing the concept.

Those five factors—solves a problem, tests something new, challenges the status quo, is collaborative, and is measurable—comprise a good experiment. An experimenter's ability to stay agile and flexible makes an even better experiment. Experiments may not always move in the intended direction, or you may learn something that requires you to pivot, so staying flexible and adjusting experiments is essential in the long run. For example, I have experimented with library displays, which traditionally showcased unique materials from special collections. We tracked how many people visited the display daily. At one point, a library user inquired about curating an exhibit of zines. Although not a library resource, the idea seemed worth testing. The number of visitors increased significantly, so I asked the user if he had any other objects to display, and he enthusiastically shared his miniature toy and figurine collection. This exhibit was by far the most popular we had displayed and helped me pivot toward thinking of library displays as attractions instead of advertisements. Future exhibits included Indigenous cultural artifacts and Bauhaus-inspired architectural objects. Again, this agility to quickly change directions supports the experimental mindset. Experimentation is more about being open to ideas than methodically testing ideas, and the examples in the chapter highlight this attitude and way of thinking.

Beta Spaces

Library experiments can take various forms but as previously mentioned generally come into fruition as technology-, program-, or space-based. Given the usual limitations on library space, space-based experiments always prove valuable and compelling. These beta spaces serve as a mechanism to test the most effective and efficient use of a library's footprint. The article "Making Room for Innovation" discusses two space experiments, the Chattanooga (Tennessee) Public Library 4th Floor and the Labrary, a pop-up space in Cambridge, Massachusetts.[1] Both show how library spaces can be adapted when necessary and framed as experiments.

In 2013, the Chattanooga Public Library transformed a 12,000 square foot storage area of its downtown branch into a lively community makerspace and civic commons.[2] The idea was not only to repurpose the building's fourth floor but use it as a space to prototype ideas and new initiatives. After experimenting with various iterations, the library could test ideas on this floor and deploy successful models to other library departments. It serves as a public test lab for local individuals, entrepreneurs, and artists to experiment with high-tech and low-tech gadgets like hand tools, vinyl plotters, 3D printers, laser cutters, and the like. However, the space called the 4th Floor does more than make these technologies available; it supports programming around the technologies to showcase its uses. The library partnered with AIGA (www.aiga.org), a professional design organization, on a maker day expo to introduce many types of 3D technology, including hobbyist machines, large-scale industrial models, 3D scanners, and an experimental 3D video conferencing system.

Through its transformation and events like the maker day expo, the 4th Floor operates as a space to implement new ventures, but more so, a tool to transform library culture. It entrenches the library as a part of maker culture and a place to tinker with new ideas. The space design was highly flexible and responsive to user needs. Everything is reprogrammable, from movable elements like partitions to powerful, high-impact digital tools. It is a place to test and refine service models, and then changes can be rolled out to other library departments with less disruption.

Another space transformation is the Labrary, which occupied a vacant storefront one block from Harvard Square for thirty-seven days.

The temporary space operated as a public gallery of Harvard's Graduate School of Design (GSD) students' projects on the future of libraries.[3] The space invited the public to interact with the projects or sit and get work done in a 10-foot-tall Mylar inflatable reading room. Most of the area was unfinished and intentionally messy. The atmosphere invited people to try things and learn by experimenting—a reflection of the design school curriculum that encourages prototyping, asking for criticism, and reiterating based on criticism. It served as a space for the GSD and Harvard Library to outsource risk and innovation to test experimental ideas without disrupting the services at actual library locations.

Situating the space outside of a library meant projects could remain genuinely exploratory. The vibe was entirely different from a traditional library space. It was raw and experimental. Inside the pop-up space, the coordinators and students hosted talks, exhibited coursework, engaged in class discussion, and generally stimulated collaboration and creativity. For instance, researchers and professors from neighboring universities Harvard and MIT spoke to students and community members to foster a diverse dialog in the Labrary. A table at the entrance asked visitors to describe "the library of the future" on a Post-it, an activity that gathered data from the visitors on their thoughts on libraries. The Labrary experiment generated more questions than answers and highlighted that there is no universal solution to the future of libraries. Nevertheless, it allowed design students to deploy some of their innovations, test them with the public, and determine which ones warranted future development.

As the authors of "Making Room for Innovation" conclude, the general lesson learned from both beta spaces is "the risk of creating unprogrammed space has been rewarded with new programming and uses of the environment that we could never have expected when we began."[4]

The Library Test Kitchen

The Harvard design school course that the Labrary grew out of sought to involve students in creating the library as part of the academic curriculum. Following the course, the project morphed into the Library Test Kitchen, which its website describes as "a seminar and community bringing together librarians, students, and designers to discover innovative new programs, services, and spatial strategies for libraries."[5] Although it originated at the Harvard Graduate School of Design, it is now an online platform for sharing "recipes" or playful projects that libraries can introduce to test an idea in a new environment. The recipes attempt to build library products, create library experiences, or pilot a library service, within a model of experimentation. Not every library has the luxury of a vacant storefront or 12,000 square-foot storage area. Instead, the recipes are micro-projects that can be implemented quickly and efficiently. In the spirit of keeping projects participatory, there is a feature on the website to "Add Recipe" if you have an experiment to contribute.

Examples of experiments in the Library Test Kitchen include Wi-Fi proof booths, spaces for young people to interact with technology of the past, and digital campfires for charging devices. Each project consists of a brief description and step-by-step directions. For instance, the Wi-Fi Cold Spot is a space to disconnect from the internet and focus on productivity. To create such a space in your library, there are five-step directions. Essentially, craft a wood box and paint it with EMV-shielding paint to block cellphone and Wi-Fi signals, furnish the interior with dim lighting and a beanbag, and finally, create signage using Sharpies on paper designating it as a Wi-Fi cold spot. The simplicity of these recipes makes them stand out as achievable, as evident in the Media Memory experiment. The directions include finding a space in the library with furniture that is inviting for young people, then placing older media items like typewriters, Walkmans, Polaroid cameras, and cassette tape players. It further suggests creating a board where young people can post the work they have created. An experiment on the more extravagant side is the Electric Campfire, but the underlying idea is simple, a mobile box for library users to hover around while their devices charge (figure 6.1). It involves some effort to assemble the guts—a switch box, outlet, marine RV battery, converters, and such. In the end, you have a movable box that you can place in various locations around the library that generate the communal atmosphere of a campfire.

Experiments at the University of Toronto Libraries

The University Chief Librarian's Innovation Awards at the University of Toronto Libraries (UTL) were launched in 2016 to create an avenue to bring new ideas forward and streamline the funding process. In a July

FIGURE 6.1 Electric Campfire / PHOTO BY JENNY HONG, 2013

2022 interview with the author, Laura Anderson, director for strategic initiatives at UTL, described how the university's chief librarian, Larry Alford, developed the awards as a way for anyone in UTL to bring forward new ideas regardless of rank or supervisory responsibilities. Further, as part of a larger cultural shift, the Innovation Awards infuse the traditional institution with a different perspective geared toward more risk-taking and opportunities for library employees to develop new skills. In the first year, nine projects received funding, and the awards program has been growing and adapting ever since. As a model for experimentation, the awards operate as an experiment too. Anderson, who facilitates the award process, explained that there are always lessons learned, and recalibrating year-to-year is part of the process.

In their current form, the awards operate on an eleven-month cycle. This time frame allows participants to work within the annual budget cycle and develop new skills like budgeting and project management. Further, the submission process strives to be straightforward and unintimidating. Interested employees submit a two-page proposal that addresses the timeline, budget, and potential collaborators. If advantageous, Alford or Anderson meets with potential applicants to discuss how to strengthen the proposals before submission. They talk through ideas and make connections with other interested departments across the library system to help move the submissions forward. After the submissions are received, Alford, in his role as chief librarian, reviews all the proposals. He sees the Innovation Awards as an opportunity to hear all the new ideas and cut through the layers of getting the necessary approvals. The goal of the submission process is to remove the red tape. No supervisor approval is required, and it is a mechanism for employees to bring ideas forward outside the normal departmental expenditures process. In the end, as many projects as possible are approved.

Once a project is approved, several support structures are in place to set the project teams up for success. At the beginning of the budget cycle, the project teams collectively meet with Alford and a support team to share their ideas. This is another opportunity to talk through ideas and get feedback. The support team consists of Anderson and staff from human resources and finance. The kick-off meeting covers specifics like hiring student employees, negotiating contracts, submitting purchases, and so on—processes most project teams have not been responsible for before. Then project teams are free to start their experiments, with communication via a group e-mail, so everyone can be reached if questions or challenges arise. At the halfway point, Anderson checks in with the teams and offers any help needed to meet their goals. As the final part of the process, the project teams submit a one-page report that shares how the project evolved and lessons learned, and also meet with the UTL executive team to showcase their work and share their experience. The process is lightweight and allows project teams to experiment with and explore their ideas.

Innovation Award projects range from new tools to symposiums. The awards have minimal limitations to encourage all types of projects from any corner of the library system. The only existing restriction is that the nature of projects must focus on something other than redeveloping spaces. The need to restrict renovation projects was a lesson learned from the first round of projects in which a team installed a family study space in the main campus library. Although the project at the time fit the definition of innovation and was well-received, the logistics of doing a space renovation in such a short time frame proved challenging, so going forward the awards exclude capital improvement projects. Although the Innovation Awards may seem to indulge the individual who proposed the project, one purpose of the award is to create an opportunity for library employees to explore a special interest or launch a pet project. Alford wants library staff to be imaginative and play at work, so the awards seek to operate as a foundation for people to be more creative in their jobs.

Interestingly, UTL does not share completed and ongoing projects formally or systematically. Anderson states that this is intentional, so people do not feel limited by previous projects. They want new ideas that are not modeled after other ideas. Thus, not publishing or discussing them eliminates expectations for future proposals. However, team members are welcome and encouraged to talk about their projects. This approach generates a wide range of fresh ideas. One project created online training videos that were fun and engaging. The purpose was to turn information literacy content that can sometimes be dry and boring into short, cute videos. Another learning tool created was the Toronto Film Map, which leverages geographic information systems to identify films based in Toronto. It further increases access to the Media Commons Archives, a UTL department that acquires and preserves media-based materials. Some technology-focused projects include introducing light therapy lamps at various libraries to improve student wellness, touch screens in the Thomas Fisher Rare Book Library, and a MiRo-E robotic dog at the Engineering and Computer Science Library that students can practice programming on.

A program-focused project organized data-detox programming to address the lack of understanding around digital security and privacy risks. The week-long event included a panel discussion, workshops, and an in-house expo with hands-on instruction and free giveaways. There has also been an uptick in program experiments that address equity, diversity, and inclusion issues. For example, one team hosted a symposium to discuss cultural property acquisitions, which questioned whether libraries and archives were the proper stewards of cultural materials. Other projects expanded digital access to Black literature and offered development programs on Indigenous allyship and reconciliation. Relatedly, a recent project commissioned a local artist to create welcome signs in Indigenous languages, which UTL displays at library entrances. Anderson does not describe the variety of these projects as strategies but rather as tactics to move the University of Toronto Libraries toward their strategic goals.

The "tactic" approach to strategic development is further evident in an Innovation Awards project titled the 99 AI Challenge. The project, a series of events introducing people who are not artificial intelligence experts to potential uses of the technology, supports UTL's commitment to teaching literacy, critical thinking, and evaluation of information. Further, it fits the description of the awards—projects that have the potential to be transformative for UTL and the communities served. As a cross-disciplinary hub, the library was a natural fit to bring people across the university together to learn about AI. The inspiration for the award submission is described in a chapter of the book *The Rise of AI: Implications and Applications of Artificial Intelligence in Academic Libraries*.[6] It was born out of a library interest group that met to discuss and build awareness of AI technology among library professionals. Discussions centered around the fact that soon artificial intelligence will affect the way users search for information. Given the University of Toronto's reputation as a hub for AI research and the potential impact the technology could have on information retrieval, the library was uniquely positioned to lead instruction on AI for faculty, staff, and students who want to know more about the basics.

At its inception, the 99 AI Challenge aimed to welcome anyone who did not have access to AI educational opportunities through their day-to-day work at the university. As a result, the project team received over five hundred and fifty applications to participate in the program. They narrowed the final number down to a diverse group of ninety-nine individuals based on existing knowledge of the topic and background. In Phase 1 of the experiment, participants engaged in a six-module course and a peer-to-peer discussion on a Slack channel. Phase 2 consisted of six conversations where experts at University of Toronto presented their work at the intersection of AI and immigration, ethics, healthcare, art and performance, bias and racism, and women-founded start-ups. Each event included a think-pair-share-style discussion. To graduate from the 99 AI Challenge, participants must complete the modules, attend four conversations, and respond to two feedback surveys.

As with any experiment, an assessment was critical to understanding the program's effectiveness. In the end, 48 percent of participants met all the graduation requirements, and 8.5 out of 10 said they would recommend the program to a friend or colleague. Most importantly, 97.5 percent of participants said their knowledge of AI was more robust after completing the challenge. Outcomes identified in the publication include an increased competency, a more critical analysis, and a more ambivalent perspective of AI. Ultimately, the 99 AI Challenge gave members of the University of Toronto community an opportunity to learn more about AI. Like many Innovation Award projects, this program and technology experiment had a broad reach. Although it was only a six-person team, libraries and people across the system benefited.

Like the AI project example, Anderson explained that although it is not a requirement, most projects are collaborations across departments or with units outside the library. That is part of what makes the projects experimental. In another example, the creation of a family study space, a team partnered with the university's Family Care Office to better understand the needs of students who are parents. Working with people outside of your immediate unit and with different expertise is one way to experiment. Experiments should test ideas that go beyond tasks in your daily routine, and collaborating with new people propels experiments in that direction. Besides growing partnerships, the Innovation Awards encourage collecting data in a limited time. After the initial budget cycle, project teams have enough information to decide whether to continue. Anderson said that occasionally there will be more funding when a project team will request another round of funding to test a new iteration of the project; however, once the project has been thoroughly tested and established, teams are encouraged to make an ongoing funding request through a departmental budget. The Innovation Awards are intended to provide start-up funding and allow testing and data collection, which enables teams to acquire the ingredients for a long-term funding pitch within their departments and units. Anderson shared that the Innovation Awards are a low-cost, high-impact tool. She said it was surprising how minimal the funding requests are for such innovative ideas and that the idea is to "just let people try and get out of their way."

Momentum from COVID-19

The global COVID-19 pandemic altered the habits of everyone, and libraries were no exception. It required us to work in new and different ways. It demanded we experiment. Bonnie Morley, a school librarian at the Edmonton Public Schools, wrote about how she used experimentation during the pandemic in her article *Lists of Opportunities: My Experience as a School Librarian During the COVID-19 Pandemic*.[7] In October 2022, I interviewed Morley to learn more about her approach. She explained that school libraries have a different dynamic than academic, public, or special libraries. Building relationships with students and seeing them grow is critical to her work.

Morley told me that before the pandemic, she divided her time across two junior high school libraries, spending two and a half days weekly at each library. As with many of us, the pandemic challenged her to think about what the most effective work schedule might be. As a result, she switched to a five-day rotating schedule where she alternated Thursday through Wednesday at each school. She also found more students contacting her via e-mail after library hours, and she was happy to meet them at this point of need. The changes to her schedule allowed her more uninterrupted time at each library and the opportunity to build stronger connections with the students. Morley says adjusting her schedule was the most crucial experiment because it completely changed how she worked and her ability to invest time and energy toward new initiatives at each school. The change in work schedules and additional flexibility in work environments implemented during COVID-19 is a positive step in making more time for experimenting across all library types.

With the additional time and flexibility, Morley experimented with asynchronous library services to deliver resources to students from a distance. In her article, she states that "the first change in the library started with me."[8] The pandemic forced information professionals to rethink how to deliver resources and services, and required a willingness across the profession to make those changes. For Morley, this meant building a digital presence for the library. Before COVID-19, the library did not have a website since it was primarily a place students experienced in person, so there was little need for a website catered to junior high students. Of course, COVID-19 changed that. The new website featured how-to videos, book recommendations, book talks, e-books via Overdrive (thankfully a pre-COVID acquisition), and a Google Meets link for the book club. Further, a new service, Skip the Scan, which Morley cleverly named after the Canadian food delivery service Skip the Dishes, leveraged a previously unused feature of the library catalog to allow students to place holds on items and then have them delivered to their classrooms. Placing holds on books was a new process for the students that required them to learn how to use the library system.

Morley explained that she thought of the website and Skip the Scan as experiments. As she stated in her article, the pandemic made her realize that it was time to try something new, and the risk was low. It required time and effort but no additional budget. With the desire to continue providing access to library resources and services, and the prospect of job cuts increasing the need to prove her impact, she had nothing to lose by investing in the experiments.[9] During our interview she explained to me that, as with any experiment, she learned a few things, too. Although the digital tools were helpful, the staff could have done more to engage the nonreaders. Morley anecdotally understood the importance of the social aspect when junior high students experienced the library in person and browsed the shelves like they did before the pandemic. Still, the move to only online access provided data to support her intuition. Knowing that browsing and experiencing the library with peers is critical to engaging nonreaders, Morley shifted her focus to reconfiguring the library space. With the support of the data, she sought to improve the flow of the library so that it functions more like a learning commons, and when the students returned, the layout of the stacks highlighted popular books. She experimented with different configurations of the shelving and furniture, eventually landing on genrefying.[10] Morley rearranged the movable furniture to facilitate a more collaborative and participatory environment. In doing so, the stacks functioned more like a bookstore, with the popular graphic novels moved to a more visible location, and the rainbow reading shelf devoted to 2SLGBTQ+ (two spirit, lesbian, gay, bisexual, transgender, queer, and more) resources relocated to a more discreet location. Morley devoted space to host robotics and art in the library that could double as a classroom space when in-person activities resumed.

Because of COVID-19, Morley had the time to experiment with library services and space. In our interview, she said that the pandemic made her realize the importance of making time to try new things. Even the tight budget in school libraries has not stopped her from experimenting. She looks for outside funding from the parent association, grants like the Indigo Adopt a School (www.indigoloveofreading.org/grants/literacy-fund-grant) program or the plethora of STEAM grants available to schools. She continues to be agile and flexible with the experiments, sticking with what works and letting go of what does not work. For example, Skip the Scan was vital during periods of physical distancing and isolation but did little to engage students who were not avid readers. Although students continue to have the ability to place items on hold and are encouraged to use the online catalog, delivery of materials has been retired, which is a relatable scenario for most libraries.

The pandemic was an exercise in experimentation for all of us. Every library tried something new, many without additional funding and some with significant staff reductions. Morley points out that the pandemic allowed us to shift our energy toward launching new initiatives and tackling projects far down our to-do lists. Now that the world has found its new normal, libraries have let go of the COVID-19 resources and services that no longer serve a purpose and restructured time for the things that continue to benefit users. Despite all the struggles, the pandemic was a gift to libraries in enabling a culture of experimentation. Going forward, we need to continue using this momentum to propel us toward experimenting more and more frequently.

To experiment means to test an idea or make a discovery, which happens all the time in libraries. No matter the size, experiments give you a chance to try a concept, collect data, and come to an informed decision about how to move forward. However, when framed as an experiment, trying an idea becomes more flexible and adaptable, allowing more room for failure. Suddenly, converting an unused space into a makerspace is permissible. An unplugged zone in the library is accepted, or an artificial intelligence workshop is allowed. Building this degree of flexibility into library work facilitates discoveries. We do not know what the future of libraries looks like, but we do know that libraries are changing. Redefining and realigning our roles through experimentation lets us solve a problem, test something new, and challenge the status quo.

Notes

1. Jeff Goldenson and Nate Hill, "Making Room for Innovation," *Library Journal* 138, no. 9 (May 15, 2013): 26.
2. Cynthia E. Smith, "Interview with Corinne Hill, Director, Chattanooga Public Library," in *By The People: Designing a Better America* (New York: Cooper Hewitt, Smithsonian Design Museum, 2016), 214–21.
3. Jennifer Koerber, "The Harvard Labrary: A Design Experiment in Library Futures," *Library Journal*, December 13, 2012, www.libraryjournal.com/story/the-harvard-labrary-a-design-experiment-in-library-futures.
4. "Making Room for Innovation," 26.
5. Harvard University, "Library Test Kitchen," https://librarytestkitchen.org.
6. Sandy Hervieux et al., "The 99 AI Challenge: Empowering a University Community through an Open Learning Pilot," in *The Rise of AI: Implications and Applications of Artificial Intelligence in Academic Libraries* (Chicago: Association of College and Research Libraries, 2022), 3–14.
7. Bonnie Morley, "Lists of Opportunities: My Experience as a School Librarian during the COVID-19 Pandemic," *Partnership: The Canadian Journal of Library and Information Practice and Research* 16, no. 1 (2021): 1–5, https://doi.org/10.21083/partnership.v16i1.6461.
8. "Lists of Opportunities."
9. "Lists of Opportunities."
10. Genrefication is primarily used in school libraries to arrange books by category, subject, or genre.

chapter 7

ENGAGE

The truth is an experiment is only useful if people engage with it. Users provide the feedback necessary to make informed decisions about how to move forward. Therefore, getting the word out about experiments is essential so you can draw from a wide breadth of data when evaluating experiments. This chapter provides examples of how to engage people with experiments and how to market experiments to your intended audience.

How you market each experiment or series of experiments depends on the experiment and the type of data you need to collect. One question you may encounter is whether to advertise the experiment as an experiment. The advantage of promoting something as an experiment is that it sends a message to library users that you are doing something previously untried and taking a forward-thinking approach to developing new resources and services. Further, it communicates to library staff that management is excited about trying new things. When I started a new position at a research university, I worked hard to introduce a culture of risk-taking. One way I accomplished this was creating a communication strategy around an ongoing series of experiments. The dedicated space in the library, named the Experimentation Station, marketed the initiatives as experiments. I also shared information on the library website. This twofold communication method encouraged people visiting the library to test and give feedback on a new piece of equipment and sent an important message about the library's culture.

Alternatively, there are times when marketing a project as an experiment is not necessary. When technology companies test new interfaces, they do not tell website visitors they are experimenting. The same was true for certain other experiments at this library. The Experimentation Station was the catalyst for many other experiments, but not every experiment was packaged as one. When I implemented a gallery space, I did not say it was an experiment during exhibition openings because it was irrelevant. The Experimentation Station already set the tone for experimentation in the library, and there was no advantage to excessively using the word *experiment*. If people engaged with the gallery space and provided feedback, it was irrelevant whether or not I pitched it as an experiment. When you frame your projects to potential users, the most crucial aspect is that you are raising awareness about your efforts. Experiments are only relevant with feedback and data, so invest in outreach and engagement to make your efforts worthwhile.

General Tips for Engaging People

Engaging with library users can take many forms, but a manageable and predictable approach is key. Foremost, experiments should be easily accessible to users and launched on a regular schedule. Testing the latest technology may have a place in library experiments; however, experiments that feel out of reach or have a high threshold for participation limit your user base. Therefore, keep library experiments within reach of your users so that you can engage as many people as possible while obtaining the data needed to plan for future iterations. For example, if you want 3D scanning to be part of library services, test the value and uptake with an entry-level scanner. Lower the threshold for participation so that as many people as possible can provide input on library experiments. When I tried 3D technology, I started with a low-cost Sense

Scanner. It was a handheld device that circulated with a laptop with all the necessary software installed. Packaging it this way gave library users everything they needed to get started. The experiment revealed that the technology benefited architecture students and supported the library's vision to be a space to move between the physical and digital environments. At that point, I investigated more sophisticated 3D scanning technology like Artect 3D's educational packages. Still, at inception and during the experiment phase, this technology would have been excessive and limited the number of users who provided feedback.

Although we had an entry-level scanner, not all architecture students were comfortable testing this technology. Therefore, the next tip for engaging people is to partner with a class, group, or subset of your user population. Identify which group of users is most suitable to test a particular experiment. For 3D scanning, I partnered with an industrial design course that had an assignment to design a sneaker. The course instructor was judicious about using scanning technology for design, so it was a natural fit. He required his students to scan their prototypes with the Sense Scanners from the library. Once they scanned the physical model, the students could manipulate the design in the digital environment. The students gave us feedback via a Google Form on the application and use of the technology.

With the same instructor, we also produced a promotional video that showcased the student projects and drew attention to the 3D scanners in the library. The video got a feature spot in the institution's daily newsletter. By partnering with this class, we ensured that we would receive adequate feedback on the 3D scanning experiment. In libraries that serve smaller populations, engaging existing groups of people, like students in a class or members of a community group, cements a user base for testing experiments and gathering feedback.

In addition to keeping experiments simple and partnering with established groups, routinely refreshing experiments sends a message to library users about what to expect. As discussed in chapter 5, rotating experiments on a set schedule reinforces that the library is trying new things, which may keep users coming back to try them. Most experiments need at least two weeks to run their entire course, assuming that you have testers ready to go. If extra outreach is necessary, then the time that it requires needs to be figured into the length of the experiment. Longer time frames are encouraged to facilitate drumming up interest and collecting adequate feedback. Operating experiments on the academic calendar or launching one new experiment each semester works well in academic libraries. When experiments operate on a consistent cycle, they almost self-promote because interested users return regularly to test the new experiment. A thoughtful schedule, coupled with partnering with a group of users, usually fulfills the minimum number of users needed to make an informed decision.

Use Social Media to Reach a Wider Audience

Engaging a dedicated group of people is convenient but may not be ideal for all experiments. Random testing is better for some experiments. For the 3D scanning experiment, partnering with a class designing in physical and digital environments made sense, yet it presented an obvious bias to the feedback. The 3D scanners made the student's work more efficient because they did not have to duplicate designs in both the physical and digital realms, so feedback on the technology's usefulness trended positive. Nevertheless, the input was valuable. Because the library primarily served architecture and design students, confirming that the experiment supported their academic work and aided in learning the design process was crucial. Further, the feedback could be more focused on the technology itself. In this experiment, the students' bias was irrelevant, but this will not always be the case.

To draw the attention of a larger audience, consider utilizing social media platforms. They are friendly, convenient mechanisms for reaching a broad audience as well as a primary information source for younger generations. In 2022, *The New York Times* dubbed TikTok the new search engine for Gen Z.[1] Instagram is another popular platform. Ebbs and flows in social media platform popularity are common, underscoring the importance of adjusting strategies to reach your target audience and remaining nimble. Libraries customarily use Instagram to post about new books, events, or staffing changes. However, there is an opportunity to leverage Instagram further to communicate about experiments. A benefit to using Instagram is that it can be customized for professionals to grow their businesses. It is a modern-day marketing tool. Small businesses start with an Instagram account to expand their customer base, and influencers earn income from partnerships and advertising. With a business account, you get recommendations on how to grow your following and engage more users. Moreover, you can access robust performance data to measure how many accounts are engaged with your content and what actions people take when engaging, such as likes, comments, saves, shares, and replies. In the next chapter, I will describe how I used Instagram to promote and gather usage data on an experiment.

When used effectively, Instagram does a lot of the promotion for you. For example, hashtags are a powerful tool for reaching a wider audience and growing your user base. Taking the effort to assign hashtags to a post allows it to function similarly to subject headings in item records. For my experiment using 3D scanners, I could use the hashtags #experiment #3dscanning #3dscan #libraries #libraryexperiments and tag related accounts. Utilizing hashtags increases the post's discoverability and allows users to repost and share the content, further expanding the experiment's reach. In addition to built-in marketing mechanisms, you can create compelling content on Instagram. Its Reels feature makes sharing quick step-by-step tutorial videos easy. You can use Reels to give users instructions on participating in the experiment, take polls on what users liked about the experiment, or provide ideas for future experiments. The comments section is a sounding board for feedback and new ideas.

Admittedly, if you do not have a social media account for your library, joining to encourage experimentation can be intimidating. Rob Stephens, research and instruction librarian and outreach coordinator for Ellender Library at Louisiana's Nicholls State University, shares his approach to joining TikTok in the article "Getting Started with TikTok for Library Marketing"[2] He explains the basics of TikTok, including elements like the "For You" page. Also known as the "fyp," it is the homepage where users can organically encounter content personally tailored to their interests and browsing history. Because of the algorithm, if your content makes it on the fyp, you could reach a broad user base. Following other libraries or accounts that work in the areas you are interested in experimenting with, like technology companies, start-ups, or other experimenters, can grow your user base. Looking at other account's content can also inspire you and give you something to repost, remix, or reuse, which is entirely acceptable on TikTok. The TikTok algorithm favors trends that are repeated with some variation.

Suppose you are not comfortable going all in on TikTok. In that case, Stephens suggests using it solely as a content creation platform because its abundant music and video effects make boring content captivating. TikTok content is easily and regularly reused in Instagram or Facebook Reels. Especially if you already have a following on another platform, there is no reason to start from scratch on another. Finally, most social media platforms have a live-video feature that you can use to highlight experiments in real time. These tools can use multimedia to enhance your engagement strategy. In fact, having a social media strategy and goals are critical to success regardless of which platform you choose. Make decisions upfront about the type of content you will post, how often you will post, what other accounts you will follow, and whom else you will engage. However, in the spirit of experimentation, be willing to adjust these strategies and goals as you go along. For context, Ellender Library decided two librarians would be responsible for content creation and post videos at least twice a week, and that videos would typically run between thirty seconds and one minute. Overall, library staff find the experience of being on social media extremely rewarding, especially when they post about a new resource that students come in to use because of the TikTok video.

Open Houses and Playdays

Events like open houses and playdays situate libraries as welcoming places to try new things. Hosting this type of event was my approach when I organized a playday to feature the latest technology and newest experiments in the library. Similarly, as showcased by Melissa C. Ball, Barbara M. Sorondo, and Sarah J. Hammill in "'Meet, Greet, and Eat' Outreach: Developing a Library Fair for Faculty and Staff," a chapter of *The Library Outreach Casebook*, the Green Library at Florida International University hosted an open house that set out to solve the familiar library problems of reaching the commuter population and strengthening the library liaison program.³ Both events, which are described below, provide examples of going beyond passive outreach and instead creating a multipronged marketing approach.

The playday I organized was intended to make students and faculty aware of new technology and equipment experiments in the library and establish the library as a partner in the maker experience. I partnered with architecture and design faculty and staff who worked with technology to do this. Beyond the library, other labs and facilities in the building participated in the event, which included a bot shop with a six-axis industrial robot, a 3D printing studio with modeling machines and CNC tools, and a room equipped with virtual-reality technology. In the library, visitors could test a Microsoft Surface Studio 2, the Looking Glass, 3D Sense Scanners, and an Oculus headset with Tilt Brush and Gravity Sketch software. Instead of librarians stationed near each experiment, I recruited faculty members familiar with the equipment to showcase how it could be used for design. Showcasing this connection was an important factor in making these experiments feel attainable. Much of the equipment and software had a learning curve, so I wanted visitors to have the opportunity to speak directly with faculty who could walk them through possible use cases and demonstrate the technology's usefulness in design.

Timing the playday for when most students were on campus and getting faculty buy-in was critical to a successful event. Although the playday was open to the entire community, our target audience was architecture students. Architecture classes usually operate as day-long studios, which is an ideal time for events because the architecture students are on campus. The challenge was that undergraduate and graduate studios took place on different days. Ultimately, we planned a two-day event to reach undergraduate and graduate students. It took place on back-to-back afternoons during the second week of the semester when students were eager to learn and orient themselves to new surroundings. We communicated the playday through various channels, including signage around the library and architecture buildings, the library and architecture school newsletters, and the university's daily news e-mail.

Further, by partnering with staff and faculty in the school, each group communicated the event to their respective networks. Following the event, the use of library technology and the experiments measurably increased. Most importantly, some faculty we had yet to partner with sought out the library afterward to collaborate on the maker experience. The following year, we added new equipment like sewing machines and lendable toolkits to our resources and became an active partner in extending the maker experience beyond the labs inside the building. To generate comments about experiments and develop new ideas, consider hosting a playday once or twice a year as a forum to experiment and provide feedback.

The Green Library at Florida International University regularly hosts an open house modeled after the vendor fairs that typically go on during regional and national library conferences. The open house highlights various library resources and services at stations throughout the library, akin to the library playday featuring new technology and equipment. The open house, however, is planned months in advance with a task force of four librarians and a budget of up to $500. Volunteers from the library staff each table, including a welcome table. Finding the right volunteers is essential to the event's success. Selectively choosing volunteers with welcoming personalities who are approachable and knowledgeable ensures attendees get the most from the experience. To further engage attendees, they are issued a passport and receive a stamp at each station. In addition to the passports, the event offered other swag, such as vendor promotional materials, goodie bags, food and drinks, and door prizes.

The open house ran for three hours in its first year and welcomed twenty-eight attendees. Word about the event spread because attendance tripled in the second year and reached eighty in the third year. In addition to word of mouth, the Green Library asked liaison librarians to communicate to their subject areas, posted information about the event in the university newsletter, distributed flyers, updated digital signage, utilized social media channels, and sent e-mail reminders. Smartly, they also advertised at new faculty and student orientations and secured an e-mail invite from the provost. After the event, they sent an anonymous survey to attendees that showed they found the event engaging and enjoyed meeting liaisons face-to-face and learning about new library resources and services. With this feedback, they successfully advocated to the administration for an increase in funding and expanded the event to include a second branch library.

Other takeaways from the Green Library are to take pictures to document the event and to consider accessibility issues. For an event that seeks to encourage experiments, photographs showing people engaged with them can be used for future promotional materials or to strengthen requests for more support and funding. Likewise, ensuring the event is accessible and enjoyable for all community members is essential. The location and spacing of stations so that they are accessible to people with disabilities are critical for inclusive environments like libraries. Finally, collecting feedback at each station is helpful, because participants can give raw feedback while they are in the moment of the experiment, and you can collect separate data for each experiment.

Build Partnerships outside the Library Walls

Working collaboratively is essential to library outreach efforts, and experiments are no exception. Finding internal or external partners, for example, partnering with a class to test the 3D scanning equipment, not only expands the reach of the experiment but aligns the library as a collaborative partner and community builder. In the context of experimentation, libraries should operate outside of silos and demonstrate that they are working with partners and communities to solve real user problems.

Set the foundation for partnerships in the ideation or design phases by outlining who the key stakeholders and potential collaborators for the experiment are and including them in brainstorming sessions. Working primarily as the director of architecture libraries, my go-to partners are usually architecture faculty who can help rally students to test the experiments, and, on occasion, I partner with other library directors or departments with expertise in areas where I am thinking about experimenting. To determine who inside or outside your organization would be a good partner, consider who is likely to be interested in the experiment. The library digitization lab was an obvious partner when we tested the digitization process and the electronic use of architectural drawings. When I wanted to experiment with the library's role in architecture course instruction at the advanced level, I built the necessary relationships with the administration and faculty in the architecture school. Determining potential partners is directly related to understanding user needs. Who will benefit from this experiment? Attending community, faculty, and student meetings can help determine if an experiment interests a particular group. For public librarians, visiting schools, festivals, and other community events are potential opportunities.

The idea behind building partnerships outside your library or department for experimentation is to reach a new audience and get insight into the experiment from someone with different expertise. When I partner with architecture faculty for 3D scanning or developing course content, the idea reaches a new audience beyond those who would naturally come to the library on their own. In most cases, all it takes is to reach out to the potential partner with the idea and keep the conversation moving forward. Collaborators are always willing to participate if you can handle most of the logistics and planning. Further, once you engage these partners and their communities, start conversations about what other experiments they would like to see from the library. Leverage the opportunity to gather insight from people outside your routine visitors and experimenters.

Finally, consider taking library experiments outside the library. Pop-up experiments help remove location barriers that keep people from testing experiments. Instead of relying on people visiting the library to try your experiment, take it to them. Student unions, live/learn communities, community centers, or neighborhood events are all places to reach a wider audience. Plan accordingly and bring all the necessary equipment. Likewise, try to hit the busiest times for the biggest turnout. These outreach activities that establish the library as a community partner not only help raise awareness of experiments but are an opportunity to raise awareness about other library resources, services, and events in the user's natural environment.

Encouraging Experimentation Post-Experiment

Continuing to talk about library experiments is part of the culture of experimentation. Engaging people with experiments continues even after the investigation is complete. Whether or not an experiment is successful, make documentation available and accessible to everyone.

Do this by sharing the data and results widely. Particularly for those who engaged with the experiment or want to replicate it, knowing the results—what worked and what did not—will guide participation in future experiments.

In the past, I shared current and past (successes and failures) on the library website. Doing so identified the library as a place that experiments, helped develop a brand around it, and sought to inspire other libraries to experiment. The website had two sections: "Active Experiments" and "Expired Experiments." Descriptions of current experiments included a brief description and a reason for the experiment. Past experiments included the description of the experiment and a summary of lessons learned (box 7.1). Beyond getting the word out, the minimalist approach to the website content intentionally made the experiments appealing and welcoming rather than overwhelming, so people would spread the word and try experimenting on their own. Most importantly, it communicated to library users that our experiments served a purpose. Regardless of their outcome, we were reinviting the library and dedicated to solving user problems. Documenting past, present, and future experiments is essential to experiment outreach.

Draw a Picture and Tell a Story

A visual brand and communication materials help draw the big picture of what you are trying to accomplish. They tell a story about why and how the library is experimenting. Part of communicating the big picture is sharing your successes and failures, which can be done via the library website or newsletter. Stories are a fabulous tool for communicating the message of experimentation. For centuries humans have used storytelling to share information and problem-solve. This human capacity for storytelling plays a crucial role in the human-centered approach to experimentation. In particular, failures embody empathy and understanding for someone or something, and sharing them adds a humanist element to the library's brand. Use the library website, newsletter, community events, or even TikTok videos to share the progress of your latest experiments. Spread the message widely and relate the experiment to specific user needs.

Library X Experiments

ACTIVE EXPERIMENTS

Exhibitions: This experiment investigates the library space as gallery space with ambitions to become a collaborative art project. Stay tuned.

WHY THIS EXPERIMENT? Exhibitions spark inspiration and creativity and create a memorable experience for library users.

The Looking Glass: This experiment is a desktop holographic display that allows users to view digital models in a 3D environment.

WHY THIS EXPERIMENT? There is a lot of potential for virtual reality in design, but the technology requires the use of a headset. The Looking Glass removes that barrier and allows the user to create and view the 3D object simultaneously.

EXPIRED EXPERIMENTS

3Doodler Create+: This experiment tests technology that allows users to create 3D objects with PLA or ABS filament without the use of a 3D printer.

WHAT DID WE LEARN? 3Doodler is an easy-to-use piece of technology that allows users of all skill levels to experiment with 3D making. We are adding this tool to our permanent collection. We have two pens available to check out from the circulation desk.

iPad Apps: This experiment attempted to generate interest in the iPad apps Affinity Designer, Interaction of Color, and Procreate.

WHAT DID WE LEARN? Users demonstrated the most interest in Procreate, but the level of interest was not great enough to add it to the library's iPads. Because apps are accessible to almost everyone on personal mobile devices, we speculate that users would rather download it on their own than borrow a device from the library. In addition, experiments require a lot of publicity to get good feedback, so there will need to be more of that going forward.

BOX 7.1 Library X Experiments

For instance, some of my early research was on using mobile apps as a reference and teaching tool. When I spoke about this topic at conferences or workshops, I would tell a story about an architecture student working on a drawing assignment and how pointing them to a mobile app to assist with the assignment was part of the information literacy framework. Adding a humanistic element to my presentations, such as a story about a student with an assignment, was something most people in the audience could relate to and helped build the case for mobile apps as reference and teaching tools. When I presented at the South by Southwest Education Conference and Festival, my audience was not the standard group of librarians but rather educators and technologists, so I needed to tell a different story. The story was not about library users but about how adopting certain technologies in libraries can help researchers have a greater impact on solving global problems. In another example, the video that told the story of the 3D scanning experiment with the industrial design class was seen by a grieving mother whose teenage daughter had died in a bicycle accident in New York City, who contacted me to create a 3D scan of her daughter's shoe. This heart-wrenching example shows that every story you tell has an impact. Although how you tell the story and what story you tell can vary considerably, people always love a good story. Great products and services tell great stories, and experiments are one of those.

Crafting the Big Picture

When discussing raising awareness of experiments in libraries, it would be amiss not to address culture and branding. As reiterated throughout this book, experimentation is about changing library cultures more than it is about actual experiments. Part of that culture is adopting experimentation into your library brand. Your brand is part of the big picture and tells users what your library is about. Christina Vercelletto's article "Welcoming the Curious," which features the *Library Journal*'s 2018 Marketer of the Year, Los Angeles (LA) County Library, speaks to branding or rebranding being a holistic endeavor. Geraldine Lin, marketing director for LA County Library, advises that "rebranding is a process of examining your organization, checking it against customer expectations, finding the key group of customers you can best serve, and communicating in a way that resonates with these customers."[4] The rebranding efforts at LA County Library transmitted its new identity. It encompassed new values, a mission, a name change, a new logo, a tagline, and a massive awareness campaign targeting forty digital billboards and seventy bus-stop ads.

The scale of the LA County Library rebranding is too extensive for most libraries. Still, it has some takeaways that can help build a branding effort around experimentation. First and foremost, think about the user. Check in with your users and target your library brand toward them. As discussed in chapter 4, your experiments should solve user problems; therefore, a user-focused branding approach that establishes a clear image of your library paves the way for successful experiment engagement. As part of its new brand, LA County Library encouraged users to explore library resources and services with the tagline "Curiosity Welcomed." Similarly, I branded experiments at the Experimentation Station with the tagline "Experiment. Play. Try Something New." A seemingly simple gesture, like creating a tagline, invites library users to think about and use the space differently.

A tagline can stem from—or give birth to—a vision related to experimentation in the library. In my case, I created the tagline first, thus establishing the foundation for what I wanted users to get out of the library experiments. Fundamentally, the library experiments shifted the perception of the library for both users and staff. I wanted everyone that touched the library to see it as a place to create and generate ideas. To expand on the tagline, I wrote a manifesto to declare the experiments' intentions and motives and posted on the experiments page of the library website: "Experiments provide access to emerging technologies and encourage play and discovery. The experiments are not meant to be fully supported tools or services but rather opportunities to test, provide feedback, and improve a concept. Follow the success or failures of our experiments on this page." The manifesto was intentionally vague to maintain flexibility in choosing the type of experiments we would conduct. The tagline told users what to expect, and the manifesto explained how we would do it in a few simple sentences.

Beyond a brand, tagline, and vision, it is imperative that all outreach material has a consistent look and feel. One way to accomplish this is by creating a brand guide that includes a color palette, fonts, and layout templates. Once you have a clear vision for your experiments and the branding to market them, plan an awareness campaign for the experiment rollout. Get the message out through e-mails, digital and print signage, social media, and an open house or playday.

Creating Excitement about Experiments

Experiments create excitement around new initiatives or the introduction of new technology or tools to the library. Widely communicating about experiments helps generate a buzz both internally and externally. Getting coworkers and team members enthusiastic about participating in experimentation is as essential as engaging library users. Building momentum internally helps shift the culture in the library towards one that is forward-thinking and risk-tolerant. A library culture that supports and participates in experimentation stimulates its workers and users. Testing the tools outlined in this chapter will give you an idea of what does and what does not work for engaging team members and users in your library.

Whatever outreach method you choose, whether collaborating with partners, hosting playdays, sharing on social media, taking your show mobile, or telling stories, choose the methods that feel the most natural and organic to you. Outreach and engagement can feel uncomfortable for those just starting to step into experimenting and implementing new concepts in libraries. As with any part of experimentation, adjust your strategy and adapt as you move along. If something is not working, do not waste time and energy on it. Try another approach instead. Engagement is about generating a buzz and creating excitement, so if you are not feeling it, there is a good chance your users are not feeling enthusiastic about it either.

Notes

1. K. Huang, "For Gen Z, TikTok Is the New Search Engine," *The New York Times*, September 17, 2022, www.nytimes.com/2022/09/16/technology/gen-z-tiktok-search-engine.html.
2. Rob Stephens, "Getting Started with TikTok for Library Marketing," *Public Services Quarterly* 18, no. 1 (2022): 59–64, DOI:10.1080/15228959.2021.2008286.

3. Melissa C. Ball, Barbara M. Sorondo, and Sarah J. Hammill, "'Meet, Greet, and Eat' Outreach: Developing a Library Fair for Faculty and Staff," in *The Library Outreach Casebook*, Ryan L. Sittler and Terra J. Rogerson, ed. (Chicago: Association of College and Research Libraries), 2018.
4. Christina Vercelletto, "Welcoming the Curious," *Library Journal* 143, no. 16 (2018): 20–23.

chapter 8

ASSESS

In addition to creating cultures of innovation, experiments add value to your organization by providing data that allows you to make informed decisions. In this chapter, I refer to the evaluation of experiments as assessment, that is, the act of examining or studying the data to determine what is useful. Assessing data helps you determine user needs and the value of an experiment to your organizational goals. According to *The Measurement and Evaluation of Library Services*, when assessing experiments, you should consider these three factors: (1) whether a change occurred, (2) whether the change was in the desired direction, and (3) to what extent.[1] Further, if a change occurs, you will want to determine the impact of the experiment on the user experience and its impact on strategic directions.

Although experimentation does not necessarily disrupt existing workflows or workloads, evaluating the data takes time and effort because of the need to develop tools to collect the data and to deal with the amount of data collected. During the experimentation process, you can expect to spend about 20 percent of your time collecting the data and the remaining 80 percent analyzing it. This does not necessarily mean that you must spend 80 percent of your workload on analyzing data, but as a general rule of thumb, more time and effort should be spent on understanding and reviewing the data because that is where the value of an experiment is derived. This chapter will discuss various data-collection instruments, how to evaluate the data, and what to do when an experiment does not achieve the desired objectives.

Data-Collection Tools for Experiments

User-experience (UX) researchers operate under the assumption that most of the design cycle is focused on analyzing and evaluating the data. The UX design cycle, as shown in figure 8.1, encourages iterations by constantly gathering feedback. Analysis includes analyzing data *from* the users, in addition to insights *on* the users. The point of analysis is to understand your users wholly. One way to accomplish this is by reviewing existing literature to determine what is already known about the users you are investigating and the experiment you are conducting. As with any literature review, you must use credible and reliable sources. Use multiple sources and cross-reference them to determine their reliability. A literature review can help set benchmarks, identify comparable experiments, and keep you abreast of trends and tendencies. When conducting this research, look across sectors to see what industries outside of libraries are testing. Follow the lead of UX researchers, who also evaluate the data collected during the experiment when users give feedback. These two primary and secondary data sources deliver adequate research data.

Primary data-collection methods, those used to collect data directly from users during the experiment, should focus on immediate feedback. In most situations, the users studied are those who participate in the experiment. If you need to recruit participants, reference the examples in chapter 7. Quick feedback is an integral part of the experimentation process that enables you to make changes for the next iteration of the experiment. You can collect this type of feedback through both qualitative and quantitative methods. The examples in this chapter—using surveys or questionnaires, observational studies, interviews or focus groups, usability testing or web analytics, and social media—are ideal for

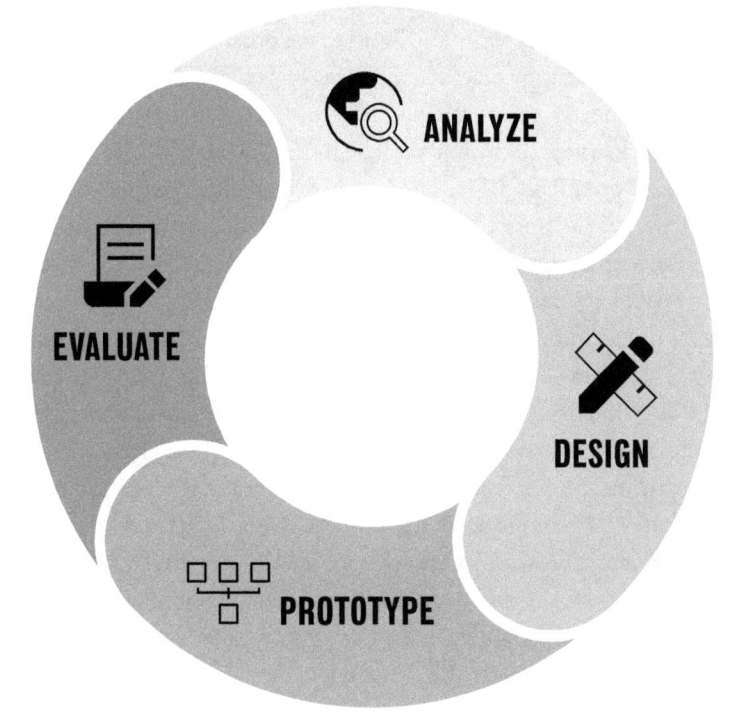

FIGURE 8.1 User experience research lifecycle
ADAPTED FROM: YANY GRÉGOIRE AND SYLVAIN SÉNÉCAL, UX RESEARCH, HECMONTRÉALX, 2021

experimentation because they allow you to gather data quickly and with minimal effort, without straining existing workloads.

Questionnaires and Surveys

When composing questionnaires or surveys to gather feedback, keep it simple by focusing on the experience of what it felt like to participate in an experiment. The first experiment I conducted in a library included a Google Form with five questions assessing the current experiment and asking for input on future experiments. Although asking five questions initially seemed reasonable, because students were testing the experiments while completing their academic work, the response rate was low. In future iterations, I reduced the survey to one question, "what did you think of the experiment?" and three possible responses: sad face, neutral face, and happy face. The number of people submitting feedback increased by nearly 300 percent.

What I learned, and what the UX literature supports, is only to ask close-ended questions. Close-ended questions allow people to respond quickly. Everyone's time is valuable, so the easier it is for users to respond, the better. Some form of Likert scale questionnaire is an excellent tool for gauging user experience. The visual aspect of sad, neutral, and happy faces makes it quick and easy for users to respond. You can distribute surveys on digital platforms like Google Forms or Microsoft Forms or in an analog format. A printed survey near the experiment immediately engages the user and requires little extra effort. Alternatively, a whiteboard where people can write their thoughts near the experiment's location serves a similar purpose. Prompt users with the question "what did you think of the experiment?" written on the whiteboard. Then provide different face stickers to stick on the board and leave space for open-ended feedback.

Designing a questionnaire or survey should be simple. Ask as few questions as possible to get the required feedback and make it simple for users to respond. Finally, use standardized questions to track progress over time. If you are testing different iterations, use the same questions throughout to gauge how the experiment is progressing. You can also use the same questions across experiments to see how they compare.

Observations

Observational studies are based solely on what you observe and therefore require little additional effort other than building in dedicated time to make the observations. As library users interact with the experiment, you can describe how they are responding to the experiment. The main advantage of this type of data collection is that the user is uninterrupted and unprompted while they engage with the experiment, so that the observer witnesses a natural interaction. Observations can be used with any experiment but work particularly well for space experiments in which you seek to understand how users use the library environment. You can also observe how they use technology or a physical resource.

In observational studies, it is best practice to obtain the user's permission by asking directly or using signage stating they may be observed for research purposes.

Before starting the observation, think about what questions you need to answer. They should support the objectives of the experiment. What are you interested in observing and why? For example, you may want to record how long people stay engaged with the experiment, document any frustrations they may experience, determine the order in which they used certain elements, or note the point at which they gave up. What you observe will depend on the individual experiment. You may also take an open-ended approach and instead of starting with specific questions take general notes on how people use the experiment. Either way, immediately record what you observe to document your observations as accurately as possible. One aspect of observational studies to be aware of is the likelihood of observer bias, that is, the observer recording what they want to see to meet objectives instead of what is really happening. If there is adequate staff, consider having two or three people conduct the observations simultaneously so that you can compare notes to improve accuracy and combat bias. Finally, accept any new and different ways people might use the experiment. Whether or not they use it "correctly" is less critical. Observations can be an opportunity to see other forms the experiment could take.

Interviews and Focus Groups

Deciding between interviews and focus groups depends on how much time and effort you can put into collecting data. Both are relevant tools for conducting qualitative research and are especially helpful when understanding how users use library resources and allow you to connect directly with users and gather first-hand feedback about their experiences. Because of their similarities, determining which is best suited for your needs depends on the information you seek and the amount of time you can dedicate to it.

One-on-one interviews allow you to dig deep into an individual user's experience. UX researchers use this tool to gather user insights on a website, an application, or a product. In libraries, you can use them to collect information on digital tools, services, or programs as well as websites. They are the preferred option when you seek an in-depth individual understanding of a prototype. Typically, one-on-one interviews are conducted with ten participants and vary in length between forty-five and ninety minutes. Needless to say, they involve substantial time commitments. In addition to the form of the interview itself, you must also consider the interviewee-recruitment process. To ensure quality candidates, solicit subjects with diverse backgrounds and experiences. The outreach techniques discussed in the previous chapter can be used to help recruit participants. Once you have recruited participants, the interviews can be structured, semi-structured, or unstructured. The middle-of-the-road option includes some prepared questions but gives you enough flexibility to spend more or less time on various topics. Consider using prompts that ask participants what they found memorable about the experiment, what aspects they felt were important, or what improvements they think could be made.

For most library experiments, focus groups provide sufficient information. They can help gauge the usefulness and value of an experiment before deciding whether it is worth a more extensive investment. Focus groups usually consist of five to ten participants, and each person is encouraged to share their thoughts. As always, align the focus group questions with the experiment's objectives. User-experience researchers generally structure focus groups to be no longer than ninety minutes. This includes ten minutes to warm up, ten minutes devoted to a creative activity, sixty minutes to discuss the main topics, and ten minutes to wrap up and conclude. When leading a focus group, giving each participant equal speaking time, or about ten minutes per person on average, is essential to hear all perspectives. When everyone gets the chance to speak, brainstorming can arise organically as participants often build off one another in focus groups. All in all, focus groups allow you to explore new ideas and compare the differences and similarities in user perspectives.

Usability Tests and Web Analytics

Quantitative research methods like usability tests and web analytics can help balance the data collected through the qualitative methods of interviews and focus groups. Both methods are popular tools among UX researchers, but quantitative methods offer usage metrics especially relevant when conducting technology experiments and testing new digital interfaces. An experiment I ran that used usability tests was with a tools portal for architecture students. The digital portal identified maker technology and equipment in various locations across the campus. The project aimed to give students easier access to tools like 3D printers, virtual-reality equipment, visualization software, and other technologies. The experimentation team was comprised of one librarian, one faculty member, and two graduate students. We met every two weeks to test new iterations and review feedback. When needed, the graduate students would conduct usability tests in between our scheduled meetings. They asked their classmates to complete simple tasks, such as finding the building name and room number for the laser cutter. They recorded how long it took participants to complete a task and identified any changes that would improve the user experience. At our next meeting, we discussed the feedback and made necessary changes. This type of data gathering offered a no-cost, low-bar method of collecting feedback. Usability testing does not require a formal lab, but if you have access to recording equipment or more advanced tools like eye-tracking software, you could explore using these tools to enhance the data and results.

For digital experiments, you can often gather quantitative data from website analytics. Website analytics primarily answer three questions: who are the users, how did the users reach your website, and what do users do on your website? Combining this data with qualitative data from the other methods mentioned gives a holistic view of whether the experiment meets the objectives and also identifies lingering problems. If, for example, we recognize that users are not clicking beyond the home page on our tools portal, we could make the correlation that they are not quickly finding the needed information. This, combined with the data from usability tests, helps us to identify the problem. Back-end analytics alone will tell you what is happening, but not why, so combining both methods provides the best investigative approach.

Writing the Narrative with Social Media

The methods discussed above present options for collecting quantitative and qualitative data. Quantitative data is usually more fact-based, while qualitative data will be based on a user's experience. Combining both methods is the best way to get a complete picture of your experiment. Another option to gather qualitative data is on social media platforms. Although analyzing social media may not always yield the most factual data, this can help write the story about your experiment. User-experience storytelling is a communication tool that can boost outreach efforts and help you understand how users use the experiment. It is a natural way for users to share feedback and attract new users; later, you can incorporate how people interacted with an experiment on social media in a pitch for more funding and support.

When I experimented with a 3D modeling tool called the 3Doodler, I asked students to share their creations using an Instagram hashtag. I was curious whether this tool would be a valuable addition to the library's equipment and tool lending program. By seeing what the students were creating, I could partially understand if it contributed to their research and learning. A short survey complemented the Instagram hashtag. By diversifying the data-collection methods, I gathered different data types and created a complete picture of how students used the 3Doodler. The benefit of the social media hashtag is that it is likely something students are already engaged with and creates a visual story about how they use the experiment. Encouraging the sharing of photos gives you a chance to reflect on how users use the experiment while doubling as a promotional tool. A visual story is a powerful tool to communicate the narrative about experiments in the library.

Diversify data collection by using multiple methods to gather the most accurate and authentic data. Whichever method you choose—surveys, observations, focus groups, usability tests, or storytelling—pick the techniques that gather the most relevant information using the least amount of work. Note also that user demands are rapidly changing, and they might only be able to articulate some of their needs. Qualitative methods like surveys and focus groups might not reflect their actual behavior. This incomplete perception is another reason to combine qualitative and quantitative data-collection methods. Further, not all impact can be measured by data. Occasionally, one astonishing story about how an experiment changed the way a user solved a problem is enough to justify its existence, regardless of what the other data shows.

Evaluation Methods for Experiments

The evaluation and implementation of data offer the most value in experimentation. An evaluation plan is critical to understanding how people use the experiment, its impact, and how to improve the experience. User-experience designers use a type of evaluation called formative evaluation, which entails assessing experiments at each stage and using the resulting information to feed the design process. In the same way, evaluating enables you to adapt library experiments quickly and make informed changes based on the data. A formative evaluation plan should align with the strategic goals of the experiment. For example, the 3Doodler experiment sought to align with curricular learning objectives in the architecture school. Through survey responses and Instagram posts, I determined that the 3D modeling tool was valuable in supporting students' coursework and as part of the learning process. Recall that I was not interested in how many people used the device. Instead, I was more interested in the quality of the experience. It was more important if one student used it to create an architectural model than if fifty students used it to create bracelets. Thus, understanding the strategic goals of an experiment is critical to an accurate evaluation.

Once I determined the experiment met the primary objective, I could dig deeper into the data to determine how to improve it. One comment repeatedly expressed in the feedback survey responses was the desire to borrow the 3Doodler instead of being required to use it in the library. This feedback informed the next iteration of the experiment. We purchased two additional 3D pens to have three available to lend and experimented with different models of access to the filament they used. We tested three lending models: (1) requiring users to purchase filament, (2) lending basic white, PLA filament, or (3) lending a variety of filaments. Based on circulation data and having the funds in our annual budget, we ultimately decided to lend a variety of filaments with the 3Doodler. The data showed a higher circulation rate with various filaments, but our decision also factored in the budget and the library's mission and vision. The overall cost was minimal—further, the practice aligned with the free 3D printing service offered at the main library.

Methods by Data-Collection Type

Data-collection tools offer differing degrees of evaluation features. Many survey tools, like Qualtrics and SurveyMonkey, automate evaluation with features that allow you to specify that raw data be converted into visual formats like charts, graphs, or word clouds. Powerful filtering features and crosstab reports aid in making correlations between responses. Tableau, the most popular end-to-end data analytics platform, allows you to visualize, analyze, and share your analysis easily. Although most online survey tools offer some automatic visualizations, other data-collection methods require more insight and expertise. Suppose you plan on making experimentation an integral part of your organization's processes. Investing in software like Tableau and the necessary training to use the tool effectively and efficiently is worth it, but you can pilot the free public version and take advantage of tutorials on LinkedIn Learning for a reduced cost.

Following best practices like systematic note-taking when conducting observations, interviews, or focus groups, makes the evaluation phase run smoothly. For observations, this means preparing an observation grid in advance (see figure 8.2). The grid should outline exactly what you are observing. For example, how long has someone used the 3Doodler, when do they struggle or become frustrated, and what do they do with the 3D object when they finish? Using an observation grid keeps observers on track and encourages them to reflect on their observations. It offers a systematic observation approach, ensuring you observe the same aspects for each user and make a fair comparison. Developing a grid and recording observations on principal concepts results in a more balanced data-collection method.

Likewise, questions for interviews and focus groups can be predetermined, with the option to be adapted on the fly if you employ a less structured format. Open-ended questions geared toward participants' experiment use are more reliable than leading questions. For example, use questions like "how was your experience with the 3Doodler?" instead of "did you find the 3Doodler difficult to use?" In the focus group setting, create a discussion guide before the interview to gear the conversation toward your strategic objectives. Key stakeholders should collaborate on this to ensure you address all areas of interest. The discussion should center

OBSERVATION GRID: 3Doodler Experiment

Date:	Start Time:	Stop Time:
AREA OF OBSERVATION	**NOTES**	
Type of User Are they a student, faculty, or member of the public?		
Behavior How are they using the technology? Do they use other library resources?		
Context What else is happening in the library? Is it busy?		
General Mood Are they happy, or frustrated? What caused mood changes?		
Other Observations		
Reflexive Comments		

FIGURE 8.2 Observation grid

around open-ended questions like those used in a one-on-one interview, and you may want to use images or mock-ups to fuel the conversation. As with observations, creating a grid based on the discussion guide ensures you record the responses related to your strategic objectives. Making the most of the scheduled interview or focus group time and good notes makes drawing conclusions relevant to your goals more straightforward.

For more quantitative methods like usability tests or web analytics, UX researchers evaluate data based on key performance indicators (KPIs). Unlike strategic objectives, KPIs measure the performance of the resource or service you are testing. For instance, e-commerce sites measure the percentage of visitors that complete a purchase, which is a critical indicator of the company's overall performance. Traditionally, library KPIs might look like the total number of circulations, e-resource use, or visitors. To select the right KPIs for your experiment, focus on the key metrics related to your objectives. Thinking back to the example of the tools portal, a KPI was the number of visitors who located a piece of equipment on the site and then created something using that technology. In evaluating that data, we found that the portal helped students locate equipment and impacted their ability to use it to create something meaningful and tangible.

Stay focused on actionable metrics and avoid vanity metrics that make the experiment look good but provide no insight into performance or usefulness. For instance, when I asked students to share their 3D creations on Instagram, the number of likes these received did not help me understand how much the 3D tool contributed to their education. The likes could therefore be disregarded. Especially with social media stories, it is easy to be persuaded by the number of views or likes (possibly inspired by increased dopamine levels). Keep the data related to the experiment's objectives at the forefront. Although a visual story can create a fuller picture of the experiment's impact, you should nonetheless make decisions based on the data and objectives.

General Tips on Evaluating Data

How you evaluate data influences future iterations of experiments. Therefore, guide evaluation by standardizing data collection and evaluation methods as much as possible. An evaluation guide, like the observation grid shown in figure 8.2, can easily be recreated based on the objectives of an individual experiment. Tools like this help compartmentalize evaluation, so instead of looking at the experiment and data holistically, you look at each aspect individually. Looking at each element independently helps keep the focus on the data and offers more opportunities for reflection than subjectively assessing the entire experiment simultaneously. Using an observation grid or systematic note-taking, you can take in-depth notes about the user: how they engage with the experiment, what other ways they engage with the library, and their mood during the experience. This specific data type differs from survey results, where users select from predetermined options to rate the overall experiment.

In addition to looking at one piece at a time, UX research commonly employs more than one evaluator to reduce subjectivity. Having multiple people (at minimum two) evaluating the data and cross-checking the analysis is essential. You must weigh all the findings, not just those supporting a particular viewpoint. A reliable method is to have each evaluator assess the data against the evaluation guide based on the experiment's objectives. If all evaluators draw the same conclusion, this corroborates the results. However, if they come to different conclusions, discussing how the data supports or refutes each objective is warranted.

Evaluating for Success or Failure

Ultimately, the evaluation process decides whether the experiment succeeded, needs improvement, or failed. What you choose shapes the next move, yet determining the results of an experiment is not always a clear-cut process. You already know that you cannot rely on a guess or your intuition alone to make decisions, however natural it is to want the outcome of an experiment to go one way or another. When I started experimenting in a library, I wanted it to succeed. Because the technology I was testing had been successful at my prior institution, I thought it would be an easy win at my new job, but the data showed otherwise. I quickly realized that students were interested in something other than design apps on library iPads. The research showed that this trend was fueled by a preference for personal tablet devices and a different student demographic that drew students from more privileged backgrounds than those of the students at my previous institution. Ultimately, if the experiment did not support the needs of the library, then it was not worth reiterating or further investment. The experiment additionally was a lesson in time and place: user needs evolve rapidly, so checking in on past experiments might yield different results, and an initiative that worked at one library might not work at another. On the other hand, there may be experiments that you want to be unsuccessful because they might mean supporting new technology or additional workload commitments. However, it should be user needs and data that drive the development of new projects, not personal preference. When evaluating experiments and determining future iterations, approach them humbly and recognize that answers might show what you least expect.

If you asked the right questions, the data collected will provide insight into whether the experiment is impactful or has the potential for impact. An experiment will likely have a positive effect when it solves a user problem. So, think back to the issue you were trying to solve and your aspirations for the experiment. Did it meet the intended goals? Do others believe it solved the problem? Did the user's knowledge increase? Further consider any unintended outcomes of the experiment. Did departments that usually do not collaborate work together? Were new skills learned? Deciding if the experiment meets the established objectives is one way to determine if it solves a problem, but be careful not to overlook the other unexpected positive impacts. Even if the experiment did not accomplish the original goal, it is not necessarily a failure. Identify how it could be reiterated, inspire other investigations, or what else you can learn from it.

Finally, when evaluating experiments for success, failure, or something in between, review how they did or did not advance strategic initiatives. Experiments that help move the organization's strategic initiatives forward are almost always successful. They come frontloaded with the advantages of infrastructural support and an organization that culturally embraces them. Although only conducting experiments that contribute to organizational goals is somewhat restrictive, when you can link experiments or their objectives to strategic plans, it makes evaluating their success more straightforward. Even when you determine you should not develop an experiment into a fully supported resource or service because feedback was not positive, there is still the possibility that it unearthed information related to a strategic goal and therefore is successful in a different and unintended way. Even though my iPad app experiment was unsuccessful, I made a meaningful contribution to the library's strategic initiative to support creative digital assets with the lessons learned.

An experiment is not necessarily a failure because it did not meet the desired objectives on the first try. Although the data may show that an experiment did not solve the intended problem, a different variation with a few tweaks might do the trick. Using the prototyping model, continue to iterate and evaluate as many times as needed. The pilot phase of any new project should be about collecting data to make decisions. While my iPad app experiment was a flop, the information I gathered about student interests was imperative to shaping the next experiment. In that respect, the iPad app experiment was only the first iteration of a series of experiments related to creative digital technologies. The iPad app experiment was the prototype and opened the door for a much better user experience and relevant library services that supported virtual-reality and digital learning.

Consider the following if an experiment does not meet the predetermined objectives. First, an experiment may be well-suited for one environment but not another (as evident in the iPad example). If your experiment failed or research shows that it failed at another library, consider testing a variation in a different environment. Is there a branch library with a different demographic or user base where it could be retested? Even another time of year or a change in outreach methods can make a difference. Before you give up on a failed experiment, consider what environmental factors might lead to success. There is always the option to modify the experiment, reiterate, and try again. Make improvements based on the data collected and give it another go. Finally, and most importantly, be willing to walk away if the data does not support further experimentation. Sometimes there is no room for improvement, or it is simply the wrong experiment to solve the problem or the wrong organization for that experiment. Know when to let go and invest your energy elsewhere.

The key takeaway in evaluating experiments is the difference between the expected and actual outcomes. If your hypothesis was correct, you learned a little, and you have the data to move the idea forward. If you thought something was going to happen but it turned out that you were wrong, you had a breakthrough. Whatever the outcome, you have the data to make an informed decision or you have learned something. Either way, it is a success.

Note

1. F. W. Lancaster, W. Lancaster, and M. J. Joncich, *The Measurement and Evaluation of Library Services* (Chicago: Information Resources Press, 1977).

PART III
MAPPING EXPERIMENTATION TO YOUR ORGANIZATION

chapter 9

Fail Forward

When an experiment fails, embracing that failure is an essential part of experimentation. Not all experiments will be successful. Being okay with that outcome and realizing that taking the risk on experiments that might fail is critical to implementing a culture of experimentation at the organizational level. Most libraries and other risk-averse sectors fear failure because the culture in the organization rewards success. Library initiatives are usually supported when they increase use or enhance the significance of the library. Measuring initiatives in this way is reasonable, but it discourages librarians and other employees from trying new ideas that are not guaranteed to advance these goals. However, that wild idea that you are afraid to try could be the biggest driver of library significance, but you need to try it to discover if that is true.

It is a common misconception that the most successful companies always succeed, when in fact there is no path to success without failure. Libraries fail all the time—we purchase countless materials that users ignore, invest time and effort in events and workshops that draw few participants, and renovate spaces with the false hopes of attracting more users, to name a few. Yet these failures are not shared widely, recognized, or rewarded. The opposite is true: they are met with disapproval, even though all libraries experience these types of failures. Instead of shying away from them, libraries should lean into them and share lessons learned more widely. What can you learn about user interests from underused books? What can you learn from the interests of those who attended the event or workshop? How can you reconfigure your renovated space to meet the user's needs? The point is not to never fail but rather to learn from the failure. Anyone who has ever experienced a big failure, including myself, will tell you that it provides more substantial learning opportunities than any of their successes.

Failure as a Tool for Success

In John C. Maxwell's book *Failing Forward*, he pointedly advises: "Fail early, fail often, but always fail forward."[1] As an expert on leadership, Maxwell emphasizes that embracing failure is the key to success. Libraries can move experiments forward when they use failure as a tool for success rather than something to fear. A shift in mentality from focusing on statistics to taking risks and being innovative is necessary. The number of people who walk through the library door is not what makes the library relevant. Instead, it is the library's impact on those people which libraries make through innovative and meaningful resources, services, and experiences.

To reach the desired level of impact, libraries should take risks and use failures as opportunities to learn and grow. Take time after a failed experiment to process why it did not reach the desired objectives. I considered the first experiment I conducted in a library setting a failure, but it never stopped me from doing more. It fueled future experiments. The failed experiment, as previously mentioned, tested design-related apps on mobile devices by setting up an iPad with three downloaded apps in the experiment area at the library. What we discovered through user feedback was that students found the apps relevant to their coursework, but they would rather use the apps on their own devices than library's devices. With this insight, we decided not to move forward with adding apps to library devices (although downloads were allowed). Instead, we shared a list of recommended apps and reinvested our energy in other experiments. Knowing that students were not interested in experimenting with iPads led us to start testing more experimental technologies like The Looking Glass, which makes 3D designs accessible without headsets, and design software like Tilt Brush and Gravity Sketch on Oculus headsets. With the insight and direction gained from the failed experiment, the new library experiments started to have a bigger impact.

We would not have moved in the new direction if we were not willing to take the risk on the iPad experiment. The iPad experiment was a low-cost, low-barrier approach to learning more about user interests. That is the power of experimentation: the risk is worth the failure, and those risks are more cultural than financial. Libraries that use prototypes and pilot projects to test ideas significantly reduce their financial risks. Additionally, if you do not take risks, your chances of succeeding are lower. Good companies embrace a culture of risk-taking. The type of "mini-failure," something that is not critical but informs a new direction, that the iPad experiment provided is welcomed and encouraged. Innovative companies and forward-thinking libraries know that trying out ideas as pilot projects and experiments allows you to identify early on what is working and what is not and that investing in those projects is needed. Investing the money and effort to conclude an idea is not worth pursuing can be extremely valuable if you take it as an opportunity to learn and grow. It is true that if you take lots of chances, there will be minor (and even some major) failures, but it is still worth taking the chance.

How Experiments Fail

Experiments allow you to fail fast and succeed sooner. Learning how to fail successfully is an integral part of experimentation. Setting objectives early in the experimentation process and assessing prototypes can identify failures before you fully launch an initiative. Using experiments as a framework for failure allows you to determine what is not working early on and adapt the experiment, or move on to the next, which ultimately positions you for greater success.

To recognize when to adapt or abandon an experiment, you must be able to recognize a failure. The most measurable way to do this is by identifying what a successful experiment looks like early in the process. As explained in chapter 5, when designing experiments, set three to five objectives of what you hope the investigation will achieve. Remember that the objectives are not necessarily absolutes, and that they require expert analysis. For example, when we tested Looking Glass, a desktop holographic display, we wanted to explore virtual-reality technology that did not require a headset and assess its unique value to the student learning experience. Our objectives for a successful experiment were that (1) Looking Glass receive a generally positive feedback rating using the assessment tool, (2) Looking Glass be used to support course assignment(s), and (3) use of Looking Glass steadily increase during the first six months. We accomplished the first and last objectives within the designated time frame but needed additional time to work on partnering with a course to meet the second objective. Ultimately, accomplishing the other two goals helped us determine it was not a failed experiment and that we needed to be flexible with the time frame to focus on the last objective. Had the feedback been negative or use low, we likely would have abandoned it.

Similarly, there is a difference between a failed experiment and an inconclusive one. We could have decided the results were inconclusive if we had received positive feedback from the assessment tool but only had a few responses. To make a conclusive determination, enough data needs to be collected. Be sure that your data-collection methods are diversified, that is, collecting data is collected from multiple sources. If the sample size is inadequate, you may need to collect more information to obtain reliable data. Consider allowing more time or revisiting your outreach methods to ensure the experiment draws enough users.

As I've mentioned, the methods described in this book were designed to be flexible and adaptable. You can pause each phase, repeat it, or stop as necessary. The phases of IDEEA keep the risk level low because they provide a reevaluation framework before proceeding to the next step. If you notice in the experimentation stage that your design could be improved, pause the experiment and redesign it. If you see that you need more participants in the assessment phase, engage more users and then go back to the experiment. That is part of the experimentation process—which is itself an experiment. Revise your plans until you have something that meets your needs. These mini-failures are integral to the process. Good experiments will guide more rounds of testing. They can be a resource for future investigations and innovative work. Use what you learn during the experimentation process to inform your next experiment. Using successes and failures as learning opportunities and means to adapt your approach is intrinsic to experimentation.

Even if the idea seems far-fetched or out of reach, an experiment is a safe environment in which to test it. Experiments do not guarantee success, but they do guarantee learning opportunities and moments for growth. With the prototyping model you are able to try out an idea in a beta form before potentially launching it on a larger scale. This mechanism gives you the platform to fail quickly and cheaply. Well-designed experiments help you assess their potential impact early in the process. When you can reach this understanding relatively quickly, cost-savings will be involved. You can try new ideas without exhausting all your resources. If you are flexible, adaptable, and willing to reiterate and improve on the fly, you will get more out of doing less.

Other People Fail Too

Some experiments fail, no matter how well-designed or solid the idea is. Actually, in the technology sector, most experiments fail. A report from Microsoft found that the success rate of experiments in the technology industry is less than 50 percent, a figure supported in the literature.[2] The report indicated that at Microsoft only about one-third of the ideas tested improve the intended metrics. That means that more than half the experiments failed. This statistic points to the importance of experimentation as a mechanism to recognize failures and abandon or reiterate as soon as necessary. Other big technology companies experience the same rate of failure. Amazon has a culture of evaluating every new feature before or at launch and has a less-than-modest success rate of less than 50 percent. With this high rate of experimenting and failing, they have failed many times.

In 2017, Amazon launched an Instagram-like shopping platform called Amazon Spark. On other social media sites, customers could post pictures of products they bought being modeled, an early version of influencer culture.³ However, criticism of Spark expressed it felt too transactional. When Amazon ended the project in 2019, it had "pivoted and narrowed the experience based on what resonated with customers." They now push the hashtag FoundItOnAmazon. Another example of a failure turned success is Amazon's dash buttons. The buttons gave customers a way to reorder products seamlessly. With the press of a physical button, Amazon would automatically order the customer's desired item and the preferred amount—an experiment in creating an entirely connected home. As Daniel Rausch, vice president at Amazon, explained, "We imagined a future where the home was taking care of itself, including replenishing everyday items that customers would rather not worry about."⁴ Although Amazon stopped offering the dash buttons, they helped customers become comfortable ordering products without looking at a screen. One last example from Amazon's rich bank of failures is Amazon WebPay. Here again, Amazon tested a product that later morphed into something else. WebPay facilitated transactions between two parties, similar to PayPal. It was shut down in 2014 but was pivotal in developing Amazon Pay, which is now a widely used platform that facilitates payments between customers and merchants.

During Jeff Bezos's tenure as CEO of Amazon, he accepted these failures without hesitation:

> Given a ten percent chance of a 100 times payoff, you should take that bet every time. But you're still going to be wrong nine times out of ten. We all know that if you swing for the fences, you're going to strike out a lot, but you're also going to hit some home runs. The difference between baseball and business, however, is that baseball has a truncated outcome distribution. When you swing, no matter how well you connect with the ball, the most runs you can get is four. In business, every once in a while, when you step up to the plate, you can score 1,000 runs. This long-tailed distribution of returns is why it's important to be bold. Big winners pay for so many experiments."⁵

Failures are not unique to large companies. Start-ups, more so than any other sector, fail. In fact, most start-ups fail.⁶ About two-thirds of start-ups fail to have a positive return rate for investors. Nevertheless, start-up culture is booming because investors understand the necessity of taking risks. Rovio, a mobile gaming platform best known for the popular game (and now franchise) Angry Birds, is an example of a start-up that saw multiple failures before it eventually became successful. In 2009, after more than fifty failed games, the start-up was near bankruptcy when one of the designers came up with the angry bird character. Initially, it operated as a side project, something to work on in between client projects and an opportunity to explore the then new iPhone app platform. Still, it was not a huge success when it launched on the App Store. It took a lot of marketing and a bit of luck when the UK App Store featured it as the game of the week before it went viral.[7] Later, Rovio cashed in on different revenue streams, including merchandising, television shows, and two full-length feature films. Rovio's history of failures that turned to success is not unique in the start-up world and emphasizes the importance of staying persistent. They would have never achieved their great success if they had given up after their tenth, thirtieth, or fiftieth failure. So even if your experiments fail, never stop trying. Like Rovio's side project model, experiments allow you to test new ideas while fulfilling your routine responsibilities. You never know when one of those experiments will be a big success that shows the impact of your library.

Libraries, too, are not exempt from turning failures into successes. Individual libraries, as well as the information profession as a whole, have overcome substantial obstacles and barriers. In the early 2000s, libraries transformed as the internet age progressed. Some of us saw firsthand how libraries that failed to embrace new models of social infrastructure lost users by prioritizing the physical book; yet, as a whole, libraries adapted resources and pivoted services to remain relevant. One critical area today where libraries are learning from past failures is cataloging bias. Methods for cataloging and classifying information are essential to discovering information in libraries. For decades, many libraries have used the Library of Congress classification system to assign subject headings to materials. However, the assigned headings are limited and biased, usually defaulting to the perspectives of straight, white men. The lack of diversity and offensive language in subject headings are becoming more inclusive, primarily due to advocacy in the profession. Professionals recognize that this was a major failure on the part of libraries but are taking the opportunity to learn from it, ultimately resulting in much more robust searching and discovery of more diverse content. In librarianship, the failure of this system was inevitable. The point is to learn from the failures and make the necessary improvements.

Implementing a Culture of Failure

In the final two chapters, I will discuss how to reskill professionals to embrace experimentation and map it to your organization. Achieving those two goals requires instituting a culture where employees are told it is okay to fail and encouraged to do so. Allowing people to fail is a magical tool to help professionals adapt to changing climates. One of the most recognized design duos of all time, Charles and Ray Eames, profoundly respected learning and failing in their office. They knew that to create quality work their team needed the space and budget to fail. Employees in their office were free to make mistakes and encouraged to fail. They were often assigned projects outside of their areas of expertise so that they would do just that. Charles and Ray Eames saw failure as a necessary step toward something worthwhile. Their practice was about learning what did not work as much as it was about learning what did. This philosophy is an excellent fit in libraries. If you are encouraged to work outside your comfort zone and told it is okay to mess up, you will be more willing to take the chances necessary to create something unique.

Further, you mustn't just tolerate failure but rather invite it. Libraries are deeply rooted in standardization and efficiency, which can deny opportunities for failure, experimentation, and innovation. Ideally, organizations operate best when there is both efficiency and experimentation. Processes to get work done effectively and efficiently are helpful, but discoveries require wandering. Employees need to know that they can spend time on experimental projects regardless of whether they are successful or not. Allowing staff to fail reduces limitations and provides flexibility in their work. Flexible and adaptable management is at the core of cultures that embrace failure. Managers should make sure their staff understand failure is a part of learning and promote people who encourage it. An administration actively encouraging experimentation and failure is critical to innovative and creative organizations. It is the only way to create a culture that invites it.

One way for organizations and management to introduce a culture of failure is to document failures and share them widely. By showcasing failures and framing them as learning opportunities, management sends a message to the organization that failure is okay and puts it in a positive light. It is important to note that this can happen at any level of an organization. Although cultures will change more rapidly when such initiatives are introduced from the top down, grassroots cultural shifts can also take place. Recognizing your team's failures helps turn staff into problem-solvers. They will see that other people have tried new initiatives or ideas and learn that they can do the same. It is important to note that people can learn just as much, and arguably more, from other people's failures than from their own. Having dedicated real estate for experimentation on your website, intranet, or newsletter and having dedicated time to discuss experimentation during standing meetings establishes a collective knowledge about what people are testing, what has been successful, and what has failed. Sharing this information and telling the stories of failures will increase the potential for future successes.

Help your team and coworkers to realize that experimenting with ideas that do not work can give them a valuable information about what can. This outlook promotes a willingness to fail. The potential to learn from failed experiments is evident in the mobile app experiment discussed earlier in this chapter. We were willing to test a technology, even though it ultimately failed. That failure, however, taught us a great deal. We learned that simply allowing users to download apps on iPads was sufficient to fulfill user's needs. We also knew students were more interested in experimenting with more expensive technologies that they were less likely to have individual access to, so we shifted our energy towards virtual-reality hardware and software. Most importantly, conducting this experiment showed staff members that leadership was okay with failure—and that I was willing to take risks, and so should they. In fact, the more failures the better. A low failure rate shows that employees are risk-averse, when in practice, many failures are a good thing if you seek to create a more risk-tolerant culture. A high failure rate indicates that your team is willing to take chances. If you start questioning your failure rate, remember that companies like Booking.com, a digital travel company, have a 90 percent failure rate, which means that only 10 percent are worth continued investment. Yet if you asked a senior leader at Booking.com if they would ever consider stopping experiments because of the high failure rate, the answer would be a quick no.

Go Forward and Fail

There is a difference between mistakes and failures. A failure is not always a mistake. A mistake is the result of making an unwise decision, whereas a failure is when a desirable objective is not met. Distinguishing between failures and mistakes is essential. Failures are almost always the result of a well-calculated risk. A failure is an opportunity to pivot and recalculate how you will reach your objectives. In most cases, you are fortunate to have failed because you can now learn from it.

Model your work on that of Charles and Ray Eames. Learn by doing. Just try it. Trust that wherever an experiment leads, it will be worthwhile. When an organization embraces failure, it encourages a learn-by-doing work ethic. Good organizations know that failure and invention are inseparable. You cannot have a breakthrough without a few setbacks. Even if nine out of ten of their experiments fail, all those failures are worth it because you achieve that one success. Discover how something failed and ask why it failed, because understanding what does not work is as important as knowing what does work. So go forth, fail—and then adapt, reinvent, and grow.

Notes

1. John C. Maxwell, *Failing Forward: Turning Mistakes into Stepping Stones for Success* (Nashville, TN: Thomas Nelson Publishers), 2007.
2. Ronny Kohavi et al. "Online Experimentation at Microsoft" (Presentation at Microsoft ThinkWeek, 2009).
3. Kiri Masters, "Here's Everything That's Wrong with Amazon Spark," *Forbes*, May 20, 2018.
4. Ben Fox Rubin, "Amazon Stops Selling Dash Buttons, Goofy Forerunners of the Connected Home," *CNET*, February 28, 2019, www.cnet.com/home/smart-home/amazon-stops-selling-dash-buttons-goofy-forerunners-of-connected-home/.
5. Jeffrey P. Bezos, Letter to Shareholders, 2015, www.sec.gov/Archives/edgar/data/1018724/000119312516530910/d168744dex991.htm.
6. Tom Eisenmann, "Why Startups Fail," *Harvard Business Review,* May 1, 2021.
7. Tom Cheshire, "In Depth: How Rovio Made Angry Birds a Winner (And What's Next)," *Wired UK,* July 3, 2011.

chapter 10

Reskilling the Information Professional

L earning to fail and experiment takes a specific set of skills that many of us already possess, and which we can learn if we do not. However, it is a different skill set than traditionally used by librarians and library management. You must be open to new possibilities and recognize when to move forward from failed initiatives. Often in more risk-averse cultures like libraries, we invest in safe projects that are sure successes and hold on to legacy projects that no longer contribute to our strategic directions and goals. The skills used to participate in or lead these projects differ from those necessary to develop forward-thinking, exploratory projects.

Throughout this chapter, keep in mind that the essential skills in progressive cultures are to be adaptable and creative. If you are willing to try something new, even when it is challenging or uncertain, you will be more successful in experimentation and be better positioned to encourage that skill in others. Much of the experimentation process involves modeling the behavior you want to see in others, be they up or down the ladder. Further, experimentation requires a tolerance for ambiguity. When you begin an experiment, the result is always uncertain, and much like librarianship, the landscape changes drastically and rapidly. Thus, creativity allows you to thrive in uncertain situations. You may not know all the answers, but being adaptable and creative will help you find them. This chapter details the skills required to be an experimenter, presents techniques to develop those skills in yourself and others, and discusses how to update job descriptions and library budgets to facilitate that culture.

Skills for Success

The people who will thrive in a culture of experimentation are those who are curious, open-minded, and eager to learn. These characteristics enable you to look for new ideas in both the usual and unusual places. Similarly, an eagerness to learn means that you are willing to learn from other areas, but it also means having the humility to admit when you are wrong. In experimentation, you will not always be correct. There will be times, maybe lots of times, when you will fail. The crucial ability to admit when you are wrong feeds into what we already know is the most critical skill—agility. Some people will point out that the management at their institution is not okay with failure, and admitting they are wrong would be seen as a weakness or lack of knowledge. This argument is justified, as I am sure many of us have felt this way at one time or another. To overcome this obstacle, show the administration what you learned from the failure and present potential solutions. This technique not only demonstrates to management that failure is a good thing but also that you are an agile employee who can pivot and adapt when necessary.

In addition to being curious, open-minded, and agile, good experimenters are also good brainstormers. Brainstorming, which requires you to think quickly, is a skill you can develop through practice. It is like a muscle that needs to be toned. You can practice this skill independently without participating in any formal brainstorming session. Give yourself a prompt, set a time limit, and start brainstorming. This exercise teaches you to think broadly and nimbly. Expose yourself to a range of ideas because brainstorming blossoms with curiosity. You can expose yourself to new ideas by attending conferences, lectures, or programs outside of your immediate area of expertise or simply by reading more. Additionally, online learning platforms like LinkedIn Learning and IDEO U offer courses on developing brainstorming techniques. Taking time to build your ability to brainstorm has benefits beyond experimentation. When you do it regularly, you may start to approach all problems with a more open mind.

Other skills that help in experimentation are relationship building, working collaboratively in teams, and the ability to analyze and implement technologies. Working in collaborative, team-based environments benefits innovation and interdisciplinary thinking. Working with others provides opportunities to build off each other's ideas and get immediate feedback. Some people function better in teams than individually, but anyone can build this skill. Those with a passion and interest in technology can learn to spot trends and implement new technologies. Bookmarking institutions doing inspiring projects is one way to stay in the know. Regularly reading technology-focused publications like the *MIT Technology Review* or *Wired* can inspire new ideas.

Recognizing which of these skills your team members have and where they need development is essential. Almost anyone can learn to experiment given the right opportunities and coaching. It can be problematic to generalize about the skills and aptitudes of employees based on the generations to which they belong, but in this context, having a broad understanding of who the experimenters on your team might be could prove helpful. Gen Z, the youngest generation in the workforce, may be more likely to avoid nontraditional approaches to work. However, if you are lucky enough to have any technology-savvy Gen Z employees on your team, offer them development opportunities to become more comfortable with experimentation. Moving chronologically, millennials have proven to be energetic experimenters. They take collaborative and impact-oriented approaches to their work and like receiving constructive feedback, all ideal qualities to have on your team. This generation now makes up the largest percentage of the workforce, so you are likely to have a few of these digital experts on your team. Make sure to leverage their skills as natural experimenters. Gen X team members generally are well-educated individuals who function well independently and with autonomy. To utilize the skills of Gen X employees for experimentation, be sure to draw on their deep knowledge base. Their expertise can prove helpful, especially when developing ideas for experiments, because they have a rich understanding of the discipline and what new areas to explore. Finally, you may not think of the baby boomers on your team as experimenters, but they are highly dedicated workers who value recognition. They want to share their ideas and have proven to be some of the most adaptable employees, having mastered several waves of technology over their careers. To produce a productive team environment, encourage their ideas and acknowledge everyone's accomplishments.

Identify the people on your team who are eager to try new things. This characteristic should not be overlooked or pushed aside. The people who recognize ways to improve and are bold enough to make those suggestions in the workplace are the most engaged employees. These are the type of people we should be recruiting to our teams. When you spot this talent, nurture it, and give these employees the freedom to do what they do best. This type of employee may be a challenge in organizations that adopt new ideas at glacial speeds, where an influx of new ideas and excitement around change can overwhelm management. For management to work smoothly with engaged employees, they can offer coaching and guidance on change management approaches and how to suggest the right idea and the right time. Ultimately, a good leader knows that these people are valuable team members and offers them opportunities and encouragement to voice their ideas.

How to Reskill Yourself and Others

In many libraries and organizations, leadership shapes employee expectations and growth opportunities. If your leadership is open to change and experimentation, or if you are a leader who is empowered to make implement these changes, include benchmarks and outcomes related to reskilling employees and adopting experimentation in your strategic plans. Setting the tone in these guiding documents can be transformative, especially when these goals align with the mission, vision, and values supporting organizational change and innovation. Those in leadership positions must understand the impact that they can have on an organization. Leaders should create a clear sense of purpose for their teams. If you have decided that part of your purpose is to ignite a culture of experimentation and increase risk-taking in your organization, then that should filter down through everything you do. Your actions motivate and inspire others, and modeling this behavior to others in the organization is the most effective way to bring about change.

As a leader, you can connect team members with a purpose. When employees enjoy their work and feel passionate about it, they are more engaged and productive, so take the time to understand your employee's strengths and skill sets. Knowing what type of work each person on the team favors helps you make informed decisions about how they can contribute to experiments. For example, if a team member gets excited about creating a vision, then leverage that enthusiasm and ask them to lead a design-thinking exercise during the ideation phase. Another team member may enjoy assessing and understanding user needs, an indispensable skill set in the assessment phase. Playing to individual talents helps leaders establish a more productive team. If you are still determining your team member's interests, ask them during team meetings or have them complete a poll to decide what projects they are most interested in.

To grow a new or sharpen an existing skill, it is necessary to actively participate in opportunities to practice the skill or learn more about it. You can organize or participate in training with your team and colleagues. Trainings and workshops are avenues to actively learn new processes, methodologies, and technologies necessary to experiment. Institutional or professional cross-training programs can have a considerable impact on undoing existing silos and sparking new ideas across departments. If your organization does not have a formal cross-training program, one of your experiments could be to implement one or reach out to colleagues whose work you are interested in and establish an informal program so that you can learn more about what they do. You can learn a lot from talking to colleagues in other departments or disciplines. There is no substitute for these types of direct observations and engagement to explore skills and ideas outside your immediate circle.

Another method to develop new skills is through mentoring programs. These types of programs are useful to help employees achieve their career goals and increase their confidence. If your organization does not have a mentoring program, consider implementing one that will increase people's comfort with experimentation. Of course, mentoring programs that pair newcomers with good senior staff will have benefits well beyond experimentation. Pairing your best senior staff with junior staff is one mentorship model, but you could also designate certain employees as experimentation ambassadors. In this model, anyone who has excelled or shown a keen interest in experimentation, regardless of experience or seniority level, can be the mentor or "ambassador." Their role should be flexible but could involve helping individuals or teams brainstorm ideas, walking them through experimentation, and giving them constructive feedback.

Another essential skill is the ability to evaluate or assess a project, and like the other recommended skills, you can hone this skill. The UX role has quickly become core to advancing ideas in the technology and start-up sectors. Many libraries are adding user-experience librarians (roles that have more traditionally been called user engagement or assessment librarians). The skills of information professionals closely align with those of UX designers and researchers. In fact, the faculty of information at the University of Toronto offers UX as a concentration for graduate students seeking a master of information degree. As librarians, most of us are well-trained in collecting and analyzing UX data. Tap into this expertise on your team to improve your knowledge of evaluation techniques. Undoubtedly, understaffing and the nature of librarians' or information professionals' work means we overcommit resources and projects may be only partially completed. Many job descriptions do not give us the capacity to include "collecting feedback" as a task, which can contribute to assessment being delayed. However, there is a high cost in delaying feedback in experimentation, so make sure that you are using the experience or building the capacity in your team to prioritize evaluation.

Job Descriptions and Budgets

Data shows that when employees are engaged, they perform better at their jobs and achieve more career success. Therefore, it is worth investing in creating an environment for employees to experiment with projects they find engaging as part of their regular job responsibilities. A systematic yet practical approach to encourage engagement is by updating job descriptions. Job descriptions and performance evaluations document what employees should achieve. Although creating a written record of expectations may seem counterintuitive when you want to foster employee engagement, including the requirement to experiment in job descriptions can encourage and motivate employees. Be sure that job duties accommodate flexibility and growth. Here are some examples of the type of job duties or responsibilities you could include in existing job descriptions:

- Demonstrate enthusiasm for experimentation and implementing new services.
- Develop new models to help approach challenges in innovative ways.
- Understand evaluation mechanisms for experiments to determine necessary improvements or analyze failures.
- Collaborate with partners and team members to solve complex problems.
- Engage in continued education and demonstrate a commitment to learning.

Building these kinds of formal expectations into job descriptions helps employees explore new ways to approach their work. In addition to modifying job duties or responsibilities, encourage your team to take time to explore new ideas, an action that fits nicely into the last bullet point. Google was famous for building 20 percent "free innovation time" into employee job descriptions. In a forty-hour work week, employees had eight hours of freedom to explore initiatives outside of their regular projects. This so-called slack time can be a significant contributor to innovation and, for that reason, has been adopted by other sectors too. The same can be true for the library profession. During scheduled downtime, you could explore ideas or projects outside your immediate responsibilities, engage in professional development, or take care of the time-consuming tasks that can slow down experimentation, like planning design-thinking activities or writing grants to secure funding.

Regardless of how you spend the time, the point is that you have more flexibility and freedom in your schedule to accomplish things outside of your routine activities.

Time commitments will always be an obstacle for library professionals who are usually over-committed and understaffed. At the same time, there is a tendency in libraries to hold onto job responsibilities or services that have been long-standing, even if there are better uses for a person's time and skill set. Establishing flexibility in position descriptions and schedules supports creativity and drives employees to contribute more meaningfully. Revisiting job descriptions with a critical eye can help you identify where there is potential to carve out time for creative work. Ideally, you can dedicate five to ten percent of a job description to working on research projects, prototypes, and experiments. Believe it or not, when employees do not feel stuck doing routine tasks, they function more efficiently, freeing up time to devote to experimentation.

Related to updating job descriptions, look closely at your existing hiring practices to ensure that you are equipping your team with the most well-rounded skill set for experimentation. Hiring people with experience slightly outside of the responsible duties can push your team in different and exciting directions. New hires are among the best ways to invigorate your organization and introduce new ideas. But hiring creative individuals and expecting them to implement innovative ideas only works when the culture welcomes it. In the spirit of experimentation, be flexible with job requirements. The Massachusetts Institute of Technology Libraries included this statement in one of their job postings: "We expect the candidate to be stronger in some qualifications listed above than others; we are committed to helping our future colleague expand their skills, as well as learning from their areas of strength." Approaching job searches with this outlook helps you consider candidates who can bring unique perspectives to your organization. Diversifying your team's perspective is equally as critical. Add new team members from different backgrounds who can offer and celebrate different viewpoints.

Organizations can support skill-building and experimentation by dedicating a fixed portion of the annual budget to these efforts. Thoughtful managers understand the need to balance projects and initiatives of different scales when allocating resources. A small percentage of modest resources dedicated to experiments goes a long way. As the leader of a branch library, I have set aside about two percent, or roughly $1,500, of the annual budget to acquire sandbox technologies, conduct user studies, and spread the word about current experiments. This amount has funded approximately two to three experiments a year, depending on the cost of the technology and equipment. Including a line item dedicated to experimentation in your budget means that the library administration follows the example of venture capitalists who invest in creative initiatives. In addition to having a budget for experimentation, professional development should be an organization's top priority. Ideally, libraries offer enough financial support for all employees to attend at least one discipline-specific conference and one event outside their discipline annually for all employees. Tight budgets in libraries can make securing this amount of funding a challenge. Still, whenever possible, managers should protect and advocate for professional development budgets because they serve as one of the primary avenues for idea development. Take advantage of the many digital professional development opportunities offered online or asynchronously, which can provide valuable learning opportunities without incurring travel costs.

When funds are limited, it is hard to dedicate even a small portion to experiments with unknown outcomes, and libraries generally struggle to manage these short-term losses. Nevertheless, short-term losses can turn into long-term gains. Over three years, my team experimented with 3D design tools, virtual reality, scanning, mobile technology, and exhibitions, all supported by the two percent sandbox fund. Many of those turned into long-term initiatives that reshaped the perception of the library and increased use in new areas. Many library administrators are focused on the near term and incentivize sticking to the plan. There needs to be a shift in mindset. To move toward a culture of experimentation, we need to see any short-term losses resulting from going off the regular path now and then as investments that can yield long-term rewards.

Leadership and a Culture of Experimentation

Leaders are central to changing the culture of organizations. Yet leadership happens at every level of an organization, so if senior administrators still haven't gotten on board with experimentation, you can start by setting a positive example. Whatever their position in the leadership hierarchy, good leaders have the humility to admit what they might not know and are open to learning from people at any level inside or outside of the organization. Leadership is about identifying the best option to move the organization forward, even in uncertain environments, and experimentation offers a path to do that. In Brian Mathews' white paper *Think Like a Startup* he states, "Innovation demands leaders who are persistent and who can challenge the status quo."[1] People that lead are responsible for making hard decisions, and experiments can be part of the toolkit to answer tough questions—they are a tool to improve decision-making.

Middle managers are usually responsible for fulfilling goals and staying within budgets. By doing so they are in an influential position to convince senior leadership that experimentation presents opportunities for guiding managerial decision-making. Yet, not surprisingly, in a change management exercise, IBM found middle managers were the most reluctant to get on board because of their deep-rooted role in translating direction to action.[2] Any deviation from this objective, they felt, would be considered poor performance. Pitching experimentation as a tool to inform decision-making can change this attitude. The best middle managers to do this are those with the humility and confidence to admit what they do not know and offer forward-thinking suggestions to test ideas in uncertain landscapes.

Traditionally, leaders aim to change the minds of followers. Some may be skeptical that experimentation should be part of the leadership toolkit, but what better way to convince followers of the need for change than with a mechanism that gathers evidence to support that need? Someone's managerial style reflects their openness or resistance to experimentation. Leaders who create barriers to experimentation prohibit the discovery of more effective solutions. Study organizations whose leadership, in addition to recognizing experimentation as a technical tool, also use it as a platform to inform managerial decisions. The latter type of leadership approach sees challenges as coaching opportunities and does not focus solely on quickly fixing difficult situations. A coaching and transformative leadership style that uses experiments for data collection and analysis builds trust with teams and ultimately creates a culture that encourages innovative thinking and experimentation. Establishing trust in a team environment is critical to support employees' willingness to test new ideas, even if they might fail. When people trust their managers enough to voice opinions and take risks, they perform better at their jobs. Successful managers know how to fail early, try again, and motivate their teams to do the same.

Many traditional leadership models advise people in administrative positions to trust their intuition. As a result, decisions that affect an entire organization are based on faulty intuition and subjective views. I will admit that, even though I have boasted about my natural intuition, through experimentation I have learned to base decisions on the evidence gathered rather than on my instincts. The recognition that intuition is not always accurate is an insight that helped to give rise to the experimental revolution and the general transition to the culture of experimentation in many industries. When looking for people to lead or participate in experiments at your organization, seek people who make decisions based on data and evidence and can shift away from relying too heavily on their intuition.

Too often in libraries, we think variability and uncertainty are undesirable traits. If a manager or employee is unsure of a new idea, it may not get any traction, so we have become overly reliant on our intuition. As a result, risky ideas face resistance (if they get shared at all) and there is too much investment in safe ideas that do not push boundaries. Any novel idea creates uncertainty; this uncertainty, in turn, is what creates opportunity. A willingness to welcome new ideas and change the status quo is necessary in cultures of experimentation. People in positions of influence can promote the philosophy that uncertainty is normal, and experimentation is a way to learn and adapt to the unknown.

As you build a culture of experimentation, keep in mind that intellectual humility and integrity are essential. Everyone in the organization should feel that sharing rough ideas or unfinished prototypes is okay. Criticism is necessary to improve ideas and push teams in a different direction. However, always focus criticism on the objective so that you maintain an environment where people feel comfortable sharing their ideas at any stage of development. Even the most engaged employees will lose enthusiasm and burn out quickly if leadership ignores or opposes new ideas. Offer recognition and rewards to people who bring forward new ideas. One of the quickest and surest ways to lose good employees is by not recognizing their contributions or capitalizing on their ideas but failing to reward them.

It is true that there are some leaders and organizations built for a culture of experimentation and others for which it will be a stretch. Ultimately, organizations that thrive with experimentation have a learning mindset, consistently recognize good employees, appreciate exploration, and are willing to embrace new leadership models.

Tips for Team Success

Creating organizations that learn and adapt is essential to experimentation. Like the experimentation process, changing the culture of an organization or team is as much about asking the right questions as it is about answering them. Ask yourself questions like how willing are you (or your leadership) to be wrong and how much autonomy are you (or your leadership) ready to give people? When you answer them honestly, these questions inform you of the needed change and resistance you might receive. Think critically about what changes are necessary to begin embracing experimentation and how likely your organization is to make these changes. Once you have asked these initial questions, you can start solving them.

In addition to asking the right questions and having good judgment, there are logistical elements that you can put into place to help teams succeed when experimenting. First, encourage team members to set tangible goals. Setting unachievable goals, even with the best intentions, can hurt team morale and the usefulness of experimentation. Frameworks like SMARTIE can help ensure goals are strategic, measurable, ambitious, realistic, time-bound, inclusive, and equitable. Beyond goal setting, offer rewards through established recognition programs to keep contributors engaged. Everybody likes to be recognized for their accomplishments, so establish a program that recognizes the most innovative idea, the best use of experimentation, or the biggest failure. Rewards not only recognize those in your organization who are experimenting but also encourage others to participate. Finally, model respectful communication and healthy working relationships. When team members see this going on in leadership or other areas of the organization, they are more likely to adopt that behavior. Quality communication and honest relationships are essential in collaborative, team-based environments where experimentation thrives.

Extraordinary experiments are the product of extraordinary teams. Whenever possible, configure teams that are interdisciplinary and bring a diverse set of backgrounds and expertise. The membership of groups that work on experiments should vary. Rotating people between teams keeps ideas fresh and establishes new connections. When designing teams, you can take a project-based approach by inviting people based on what their skills and knowledge can add to the project, or a collaborator-based approach by arranging people that you think work exceptionally well together or bring an interesting perspective to the team. Whatever you decide is the best approach, do not let teams get stagnant. The more you mix people from across departments or the organization, the better.

Finally, recognize that changing a culture or implementing experimentation into your workflow does not have to be a daunting process. The real purpose of experimentation is to make your work more exciting and less effortful. Take advantage of the resources that are available to you. If you have trouble imagining how to start a culture shift, you can always look to training or consultants to guide you. Trainings that focus on listening and communication skills for leaders or that focus on encouraging employees to share ideas in a safe environment can help create more inclusive cultures. I have collaborated with both small and large library organizations to discover opportunities for experimentation and map a plan to implement this type of work, using techniques which are shared in the next chapter.

Notes

1. Brian Mathews, "Think Like a Startup: A White Paper to Inspire Library Entrepreneurialism," *VTechWorks*, 2012.
2. IBM Institute for Business Value, "Making Change Work . . . while the Work Keeps Changing," *Executive Report*, 2014, www.ibm.com/thought-leadership/institute-business-value/en-us/report/making-change-work.

chapter 11

The Experimentation Roadmap

We are at the beginning of an experimentation revolution. Technology companies and start-ups have adopted experimentation into their workflows, and more recently, libraries and similar institutions have become interested in doing so. Seemingly overnight, access to online platforms and data-collection tools has fueled the revolution. Technology companies have the advantage of having innovation built into their infrastructure. In most cases, the company's success depends on being innovative, so it is encouraged at all levels. Libraries' biggest challenges in becoming an experimentation organization are bureaucracy and risk aversion. Library initiatives remain relatively safe, and multiple levels of approval are usually needed when launching new ideas. These hierarchical and governance strictures in such organizations make rapid adaptation of experimentation difficult—but not impossible. Pitching experimentation as a mechanism to help the organization grow and achieve its goals is vital. This chapter lays out a roadmap to guide you when implementing experimentation at your organization. It is not necessarily a straightforward path, so patience and persistence are key.

The Roadmap

To be successful, you must weave experimentation into workflows across the organization, yet there is no magic solution or single action that will make this happen. On the contrary, instilling it throughout multiple layers of your organizational structure is necessary. However, it is possible to tweak processes within your existing organizational structure using existing staff and resources, and you can do this at relatively low (or no) cost.

Before we discuss the roadmap, let us first review the fundamental stages of becoming an experimentation organization. The exciting news is that you have almost completed the first stage, which is general awareness. Reading this book gave you an awareness and understanding that experimentation matters and suggested some ideas of what experimentation might look like in your organization. With this realization, you are ready to move to the next stage, adopting the framework and tools outlined in this chapter and what we've looked at throughout the book. Because we are talking about experimentation, play with what works best for your organization and rethink and reiterate when warranted. Eventually, after you have begun experimenting with experimentation, you will move to the final stage, commitment. At this point, you will widen the scope and access to tools by allocating resources and changing the organization's DNA. The roadmap outlined below will help you move through the three stages of awareness, adoption, and commitment.

The roadmap serves as a tool to help identify areas and processes in your organization that you can modify to add experimentation. The four basic areas covered are implementing a submission process, tools to aid experimentation, establishing a communication plan, and modifying team dynamics (see figure 11.1). Retooling these areas to align with experimentation establishes a solid foundation for success and innovation. You can implement elements of these four areas in unison. All the parts move together to develop a system for supporting experimentation

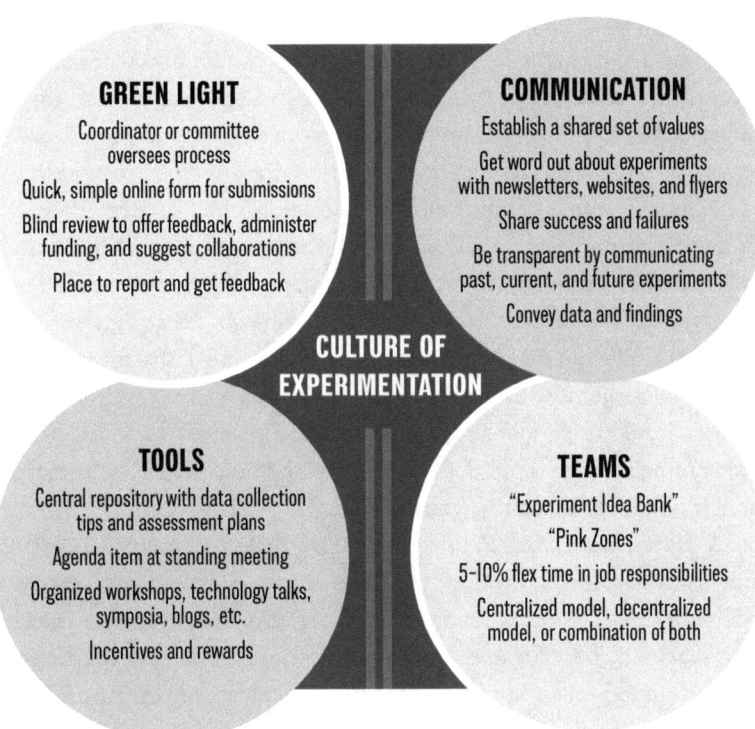

FIGURE 11.1 The roadmap

and inspiring a culture shift. The suggestions and ideas shared in each section below are not exhaustive but can provide a launching point.

The Green Light

The first part of the roadmap is a process for employees to get quick approval and buy-in from the administration. A formal but easily navigated process helps to engage experiment experts in the organization, gather feedback, and report results. A central body made up of an experiment coordinator or committee can be an ambassador for all things experiments in the organization. Whether the coordinator or committee model best fits your organizational structure, people in these positions should regularly rotate to keep the work fair, unbiased, and ensure that fresh eyes are brought into the process. This aspect of the roadmap is strategically titled the green light layer because the point of the ambassadors is not to police the process but, more importantly, to empower employees at all levels to engage in experimentation. The process should automatically convey approval and focus on constructive feedback. To make the process more encouraging, managers and senior leaders should be removed from the approval process, giving the organization the green light for experimentation. Thus, proposing experiments is less of an obstacle when the administration indicates the desire for proposals and removes themselves from the rest of the structure. The submission process should be simple and straightforward with few to no barriers. A basic online form to input details and learning objectives for the experiment is all that is necessary (see figure 11.2).

A *Harvard Business Review* article outlines the process Booking.com uses to propose and track experiments.[1] Individuals or teams complete an electronic form that includes a title, the purpose, a description, who will benefit, and information on any related experiments. The completed forms are visible to everyone in the organization, highlighting the transparency of Booking.com's experimentation process. A central searchable repository of current and past experiments is maintained, which includes detailed descriptions of successes, failures, iterations, final decisions, and real-time information on existing experiments. Teams use this platform to monitor experiments closely, and if the metrics tank within the first few hours, they can stop the test. After the initial period, they continue to monitor the experiments, and the platform sends warning messages to the team if the data quality or metrics are off. Booking.com boasts a highly open culture of experimentation. In addition to embracing experiments that fail, they share all the details of experiments across the organization, which serves as a learning and engagement tool for employees at all levels.

In libraries, once the proposal is submitted, a blind review of a copy with all identifying information removed can be conducted. The blind review ensures that experiments are assessed fairly and equitably on content rather than personal preference or bias and that the reviewers cannot favor certain ideas over others. The review process aims to offer

Experiment Submission Form

Share details about your experiment. ---> Get feedback and recommendations.

Title

Your answer

Description (250 word max)

Your answer

Learning Objectives (2–3 recommended)

Your answer

Team Members (2–4 recommended)

Your answer

What problem does the experiment seek to solve?

Your answer

Do you require funding for the experiment? If so, how much?

Your answer

FIGURE 11.2 Experiment submission form

feedback and suggestions so people can craft the strongest experiments—it does not make decisions about whether an experiment should move forward. In almost every situation, the experiment will be approved but may need some adjustments before it is ready to be tested. One caveat is that experiments must test new ideas or build upon existing initiatives. Proposals that are essentially regular day-to-day activities are not considered experiments, and not moving forward with these such proposals is a rational decision. Otherwise, everyone and every experiment should be given a chance, which is why providing feedback is the central focus of the submission and approval process.

In addition to suggesting improvements, the coordinator or committee can administer funding, facilitate collaborations, and evaluate results. Part of the submission process includes requesting funding for the experiment. Depending on the organization's budget, there may be a maximum amount of funding that people can request for an experiment. Again, requests within the budget limit should always be approved although funds may require monitoring. A bonus program that awards additional funds to top experiments can provide supplemental funds when an idea closely aligns with a high-priority strategic goal. Another advantage of having a central body such as a committee or coordinator that oversees experiments is the ability to suggest potential partnerships based on their overall knowledge of existing experiments and interests across the organization. The people in this role can facilitate collaborations by introducing experimenters with similar interests and intentions.

Finally, the entire experiment process should include a structure to report the results and support for instituting experiments as full-scale resources or services. In the final stages, people should submit their investigations to the central body, which can assist in determining the success of the experiment by assessing the outcomes of the learning objectives. They can also control how this information is shared across the organization, for example, publishing successful and unsuccessful experiments in a central repository like that at Booking.com. When an experiment meets all the desired learning objectives, the experimentation team and committee or coordinator should discuss the prospect of it becoming a fully supported operation within the library. In this respect, the committee or coordinator supports the team and assists in crafting a proposal to bring forward to management for the necessary elements and funding.

Management's role is to shift the culture toward risk-taking and experimentation and to use those things to inform decision-making. A top-down approach to approving experiments creates bottlenecks and incentivizes pleasing the administration. Instead, library management can encourage experimentation by initiating challenges related to the organization's strategic directions. For example, because most libraries have increased their focus on equity, diversity, and inclusion, the administration may communicate the desire for experiments to move resources and services in that direction. Other than that, leadership serves experimentation best by sharing the overarching purpose of experimentation, establishing a system to move experiments forward quickly, modeling open-minded behavior, and stepping out of the way. The more autonomy employees have and the more comfortable they feel in their work environment, the more likely they are to contribute innovative ideas and take risks. Therefore, a degree of hands-off management is necessary for people to feel comfortable experimenting.

It is common for the most creative ideas to come from the organization's front lines since these employees often have the most insight into library users and their needs. The review process needs to ensure these ideas do not get stalled going up the ladder. Any employee needs to be able to launch an experiment without obtaining permission from management. Thus, an experiment coordinator or committee facilitates an easy submission, review, and approval process. All experiments are given a chance and provided with appropriate resources. A commitment to this on behalf of the library administration rewards the organization with better ideas and swift advancement of strategic priorities. A low bar of entry for experimentation is critical because delays that slow down work and creativity make people feel less motivated. Stay focused on the point of experimentation, which is to change how ideas move forward, essentially by changing how we come to decisions. An organization that is an experimentation engine eliminates the roadblock between creative employees who want to test new ideas and management who want guaranteed results. By framing ideas as experiments, both parties can pursue their desired solution. By conceptualizing a new idea as an experiment, pilot, prototype, incubator, or whatever you call it, there is reduced pressure and more opportunity to show how things can be done differently.

The Tools

In addition to having a submission process, there is an abundance of tools to incentivize experimentation. Some of the tools already discussed included processes of allocating money to fund experiments as they are proposed and giving employees flexibility in their schedules to work on new ideas. Still, beyond funding and flexibility, there are other options. For example, making experiments part of regular meetings guarantees a platform at departmental meetings to share new ideas and talk about collaborative work and raises awareness of experimentation within the organization. Another tool that increases awareness is a central repository of experiments. Whether or not employees have participated in experimentation, sharing proposals and results widely inspires other people on ways they can experiment. In addition, the central repository can provide access to assessment plans or templates to suggest potential data-collection instruments and tips for measuring impact. Providing a central access point for these types of tools ensures that solid support infrastructure is in place to facilitate experimentation.

Most people best understand information communicated verbally or visually and thrive on human connection, so tapping into this can ignite the desire to experiment. It is essential to take the time to explain to your organization why an experimental approach is needed. You can demonstrate this by hosting workshops, organizing technology talks, and telling stories highlighting the experiment's impact. The experimentation coordinator or committee could manage a blog, offer training, and hold experimentation office hours to communicate the need for experimentation and streamline collaborations and partnerships.

Further, a proven way to motivate people is through incentives and rewards. Programs that offer rewards for experimentation, including failures, benefit both the organization and the employee. The experimentation coordinator or committee could give an award to the most innovative or most scalable project. Actions like this that draw attention to experimentation have a substantial return on investment. If budgets are tight, rewards or incentives need not be monetary. Public recognition alone is enough to motivate most people. Features that highlight experimenters in the library newsletter or more flexible working hours are two examples of rewards that can accomplish what monetary awards seek to do. After getting creative with budgets, you may free up sufficient funds for rewards such as offering professional development opportunities to meet with thought leaders. For libraries with healthy budgets and regular salary increases, reward programs provide a platform for recognizing employee contributions. However, merit-based programs should be reviewed by impartial parties to ensure distribution is consistent and equitable across the organization. Ultimately, reward programs are a mechanism to reinforce positive morale and show people that their hard work is recognized. Again, when you recognize hard work, employees perform better.

Most library workers can only imagine having extra space to try out new initiatives and tinker with prototypes. If a library has space limitations, that doesn't necessarily have to be a roadblock. A generous space dedicated to testing prototypes and experiments may be ideal, but it is not necessary. I've discussed the advantages of having a dedicated space that library users can go to test the newest experiments. More importantly, dedicated space increases the visibility of experiments going on in the library. Even a tiny space can be configured to accomplish this goal. Space was a genuine concern in many of the libraries I have managed. Nevertheless, as discussed in chapter 7, I created the Experimentation Station by removing a public computer station. The public computers were prime real estate visible to traffic outside the library, but generally underutilized. Removing one of the computers left five public terminals, which were sufficient to meet user needs, while freeing up a dedicated space for experiments. The space was only about three feet wide but provided enough room to test small pieces of technology and, more importantly, raise awareness about experiments in the library. Even without dedicated space, experimentation would have been possible, because it can take place anywhere in the library depending on what you are testing. In the same library, we tried using the space previously dedicated to our reference collection as an art gallery. Once in the experimentation mindset, I saw the entire library as a canvas for experimentation. Experiments served as a mechanism to test new ways of utilizing existing spaces.

The Communication

Sharing the purpose and process of experimentation is critical to establishing a culture of experimentation and is arguably the most crucial aspect of the roadmap because without communication the experiments essentially cease to exist. To create excitement, you should develop a communication strategy that publicizes how you are conducting experiments. Further, widely communicating information about successful and unsuccessful experiments encourages broad participation. Taking this multilayered approach to communication creates a buzz about experimentation. It offers an avenue to share the latest developments, illustrate what worked and what did not, and find experimenters and collaborators.

The foundation of a communication strategy is establishing a shared set of values to promote experimentation and help everyone in the organization to move together in the same direction. To ensure the values are truly collaborative, invite all employees to participate in determining them. Brainstorming shared values is a prime opportunity to exercise design-thinking skills and activities. Booking.com, the digital travel company, came up with the values below.

- **Think customer first:** We obsess about adding value for our customers—guests, partners, colleagues—to make it easier for everyone to experience the world.
- **Succeed together:** We celebrate team success through making connections, building trust and valuing the diverse perspectives of others.
- **Own it:** We deliver on our promises, make informed decisions and prioritise to get the important things done today.
- **Learn forever:** We are resilient, take time to reflect and seek to learn—from colleagues, from the outside world and from our values.
- **Do the right thing:** We get the results the right way. For each other, our communities and the world around us.[2]

A shared set of values establishes a common attitude and principles around experimentation. A simple gesture like creating an "Experimentation

Manifesto" can build a shared interest in experimentation and reflect a library's values. The values can be straightforward. Our manifesto communicated two things: (1) the purpose of the experiments was to encourage play and discovery, and (2) the experiments were meant to be rough versions that people could improve upon. Stating this publicly on our website spread the word beyond the library team and engaged users with our values. Whatever your values, the reason you are experimenting should be communicated widely, but it does not need to be complex or complicated.

A communication strategy for experiments serves a twofold purpose. Internally, it explains the value of experiments to your organization, and externally, it creates a buzz around experimentation. At a minimum, use existing avenues for communication, such as the library newsletter, intranet, and website, to disseminate information about experiments. When you first launch experiments, start with a project that can be deployed and assessed quickly. A quick win can serve as an example and generally generate interest in experimentation. Further, share successful and unsuccessful experiments to communicate that failure is part of the culture. Failed experiments can inspire future iterations or brand-new experiments.

A communication strategy should be fully transparent. Access to all past, current, and future experiments and the findings, including the collected data, ensures that people have the best information possible when designing and assessing experiments. The more information that is shared, the better equipped employees will be to conduct productive experiments. To share information broadly beyond passively uploading content to a central repository, select a time to regularly schedule informal meetings where people are welcome to share their latest developments and ask questions. This regular gathering keeps people motivated and encourages the discussion of experimentation aims and methods.

The Team

In the previous chapter, I discussed the composition and skill set of the ideal team. This section focuses on facilitating team interactions and reviews team models. We know that team-oriented organizations underscore autonomy and empowerment, and that this fosters creative ideas. Giving employees the freedom to explore ideas across organizational boundaries unlocks their innovative potential. To map this concept to your organization, it is essential to deliver opportunities for team interactions that involve slight to minimal oversight from management.

Organizing teams around different types of projects that spark individual interests keeps people engaged and motivated. One way to achieve this is by collecting ideas in an "Experiment Idea Bank" visible to everyone on the library intranet or website. With all ideas accessible, people can offer to collaborate on a specific project. Organizing small groups like this to focus on radical and innovative projects allows people to pursue individual interests and collaborate across interdisciplinary or organizational boundaries. Two- to four-person teams maintain an intimate scale, allowing people to work quickly, keep ideas fresh, and inspire each other.

Some technology companies and start-ups offer "pink zones" or "pink teams" when organizing small-scale, project-based teams. They are called pink zones because they reduce red tape. A pink zone lightens rules so ideas can advance more rapidly. By design, they allow people more freedom to play with ideas and prototypes by reducing the number of approvals needed to move an idea forward. Pink zone projects can be mapped to slower periods in schedules and grant time needed to move the project along.

Creating time for experimenting with pink zone projects is one way to balance the multiple priorities facing information professionals in their daily work. In a library, this could look like a group of library workers gathering informally to talk about artificial intelligence and augmented reality. These conversations may produce projects to test out their ideas. This scenario played out in one of my previous positions. I wanted to pilot an augmented-reality art exhibit of objects designed by women designers. We had access to the necessary technology and design objects and committed some working hours to this project. The project was within the scope of my job responsibilities. Still, moving forward without asking for permission or obtaining approval was pivotal to getting the project done because we wanted to launch it in time for an annual symposium. With the art exhibit, we chose five objects to test instead of digitizing all the objects in the collection. Piloting it in this way made the task more manageable. It gave us a prototype to pitch should we require additional staff and funding to digitize the remaining objects in the collection.

In the previous chapter, I briefly discussed two approaches for assembling teams: project-based and collaborator-based. Still, other models might be a better fit for your organization. You might use the models outlined below for the groups that conduct experiments and for experimentation committees. The first is a centralized model, an excellent option for the experimentation committee. A team of specialists who focus on long-term goals and projects is put together in the centralized model. With this method, people from across the organization work together to accomplish a common goal, in our case, to implement experimentation. One disadvantage of this model is that specialists can feel removed from the on-the-ground work going on in the organization.

A decentralized model may be the better fit, especially if your organization has several departments with specialized expertise. In this model, the organization distributes specialists throughout different departments. For example, each department or unit could have an experiment expert who reports to the experimentation coordinator or committee. The advantage of this model is that you have experimentation experts in each department actively implementing and shepherding the work. The decentralized model's disadvantages include limited knowledge-sharing across departments and less opportunity for collaborations to generate tools like the idea bank or assessment templates.

A third option is to combine the centralized and decentralized models. The combined model offers the most robust distribution of organizational best practices and communication. For instance, experimentation experts from each department collaborate on a committee, focusing on the design, execution, and analysis of experiments. Ultimately, deciding what model and tools work best depends on the individual organization. Large library systems benefit because they can draw from a large staff and have access to special expertise but can face significant communication challenges. In contrast, small libraries may appoint one person as the experimentation coordinator but may only be able to commit to a few hours a week. There will be hurdles to jump through regardless of organization size and scope.

Barriers and Bridges

Your organization's existing structure and programs can help you predict what barriers or bridges you may face when introducing experimentation. As mentioned, hierarchy-based organizations present specific challenges. When ideas are implemented from the top down, it creates bottlenecks for new projects, and employees on the front lines can feel like they are only allowed to do what they are instructed to do. One way to test experimentation in these organizations is by locating them in individual departments or branch libraries. Often, these units have more autonomy and can implement pilot projects more quickly. Limit the number of approvals needed as much as possible, as bureaucracy substantially slows experimentation down. Another barrier can occur in organizations that favor employees who do not challenge the status quo. Questioning the status quo is a positive attribute of experimentation, so organizations that truly want to innovate seek employees with this trait. Reward the people who challenge the status quo. To test and innovate, find ways to value the people who are continuously improving services and resources, and who can launch projects and keep them going.

Organizations or departments that are best suited for experimentation are those that value autonomy, empathy, and recognition. Transforming a culture to be more experimental requires a change in activities and attitudes, which must be infused throughout the organization. Ideally, the administration incentivizes all levels and departments in the organization to experiment. Incentivizing only some departments to experiment when this does not occur in other departments can create challenges across the organization, so take measures such as developing an organization-wide communication strategy to ensure experimentation is equitably applied. Communication helps build trust and confidence in employees toward those who carry out decisions.

You will remember from chapter 4 that empathy, observation, and design thinking are the three critical ingredients for innovation, so instill these attitudes and activities in your library, from the boardroom to the circulation desk. Nurturing these ingredients at all levels of an organization sets the groundwork for experimentation. Use this human-centered approach to understand user needs. An empathetic understanding of user problems helps you identify areas to experiment with and is a solid investment in innovation and long-term sustainability for an organization. To build on this understanding, observation and design thinking are tools that help you take an empathetic approach to problem-solving and experimentation. These three ingredients are the bridges to experimentation.

Go Forth and Experiment!

If you only take one thing away from this book, I hope it is that experimentation is a way of thinking. It is an openness and willingness to try new ideas, even when they may take you off the expected path. Taking the time to read this book shows that you have the courage to try something slightly outside the norm, and there is no better time to start doing that than right now. The roadmap and ideas presented in this chapter provide the starting point for your experimentation journey. Sift through the notes you made while reading this book or revisit the chapters that resonated with you, then select the ideas that fit you and your organization best. After some trial and error, you may need to adapt or reinvent what you initially thought would be the best fit. After all, experimentation itself is an experiment, and the journey and willingness to try new things are the greatest rewards.

As you experiment, remember that you will encounter setbacks and failures and do not let them discourage you. All it takes is one simple idea or realization to set you on the right path again. Progress on the path to utilizing experimentation as an instrument for testing new ideas and making decisions is gradual. Cultural change takes time. It will require recognizing the need for change and persistence. Imagine if Apple had abandoned the iPhone or stopped reiterating when it suffered setbacks—the world would be a much different place than it is today. If innovations born out of leading technology companies and risky start-ups have taught us anything, it is that experimentation is worth the investment. Libraries can take what those companies have learned and join the revolution. You might not feel like you will change the world, but small experiments add up over time and can lead to something big.

Ultimately, experimentation in libraries takes more than good ideas and implementation tools. It is a change of attitude. Experimentation requires that you do not feel restricted by small budgets or limited staff but instead find ways to work within those limitations. Experimentation will provide the solution to those problems. It is about giving space to new ideas, even the not-so-good ones. Allow yourself and your team to be curious and fail. Base your decisions on data and not intuition. Empower everyone in your organization to experiment and enable them to make decisions independently. Think of everything as an experiment. You will quickly learn that experimentation has a transformative power; it changes how you see your work and the world.

Notes

1. Stefan Thomke, "Building a Culture of Experimentation," *Harvard Business Review* 98, no. 2 (March–April 2020): 40–48.
2. "Our Values," Booking.com, careers.booking.com/start-your-journey.

BIBLIOGRAPHY

Ball, Melissa C., Barbara M. Sorondo, and Sarah J. Hammill. "'Meet, Greet, and Eat' Outreach: Developing a Library Fair for Faculty and Staff." In *The Library Outreach Casebook*, edited by Ryan L. Sittler and Terra J. Rogerson. Chicago: Association of College and Research Libraries, 2018.

Berman, E. *Your Technology Outreach Adventure: Tools for Human-Centered Problem Solving*. Chicago: ALA Editions, 2018.

Bezos, Jeffrey P. Letter to Shareholders. 2015. www.sec.gov/Archives/edgar/ data/1018724/000119312516530910/d168744dex991.htm.

Blatchford, Jean. "Curiosity: The Most Important Trait for New Business Employees in the Tech Industry." *LinkedIn*, December 17, 2019. www.linkedin.com/pulse/ curiosity-most-important-trait-new-business-employees-jean-blatchford/.

Booking.com, "Our Values," Booking.com, careers.booking.com/start-your-journey/.

Brown, T. *Change by Design, Revised and Updated: How Design Thinking Transforms Organizations and Inspires Innovation*. New York: HarperCollins, 2019.

Carnegie Mellon University Libraries. "Data Collaborations Lab." https://cmu-lib.github .io/data-colab/.

———. "Open Science and Data Collaborations." www.library.cmu.edu/services/ open-science.

Cheshire, Tom. "In Depth: How Rovio Made Angry Birds a Winner (And What's Next)," *Wired UK*, July 3, 2011.

Chicago Public Library and Aarhus Public Libraries. *Design Thinking for Libraries*. IDEO, 2014.

Clarke, Benjamin. "Are You Actually Innovative? Then How Many Experiments Do You Do Every Day?" *LinkedIn*, October 25, 2017. www.linkedin.com/pulse/ you-actually-innovative-how-many-experiments-do-every-benjamin-clarke/.

Coldewey, Devin. "Google Takes on ChatGPT with Bard and Shows Off AI in Search." *TechCrunch*, February 6, 2023. https://techcrunch.com/2023/02/06/ google-takes-on-chatgpt-with-bard-and-shows-off-ai-in-search.

Dyer, Jeff, and Hal Gregersen. "The Secret to Unleashing Genius." *Forbes*, August 14, 2013. www.forbes.com/sites/innovatorsdna/2013/08/14/the-secret-to-unleashing-genius/ ?sh=635c9836361c.

Eisenmann, Tom. "Why Startups Fail." *Harvard Business Review*, May 1, 2021.

"Emergence of Experimental Economics." *Economic and Political Weekly* 46, no. 35 (2011): 41–46. www.jstor.org/stable/23017906.

Fox Rubin, Ben. "Amazon Stops Selling Dash Buttons, Goofy Forerunners of the Connected Home." *CNET*, February 28, 2019. www.cnet.com/home/smart-home/amazon-stops-selling-dash-buttons-goofy-forerunners-of-connected-home/.

Goldenson, Jeff, and Nate Hill. "Making Room for Innovation." *Library Journal* 138, no. 9 (May 15, 2013): 26.

Gothelf, Jeff. *Lean UX: Applying Lean Principles to Improve User Experience*, edited by Josh Seiden. Sebastapol, CA: O'Reilly Media, 2013.

Gray, D., S. Brown, and J. Macanufo. *Gamestorming: A Playbook for Innovators, Rulebreakers, and Changemakers*. Sebastapol, CA: O'Reilly Media, 2010.

Harvard University. "Library Test Kitchen." https://librarytestkitchen.org.

———. "Project Implicit." https://implicit.harvard.edu/implicit/.

Heath, C., and D. Heath. *Made to Stick: Why Some Ideas Survive and Others Die*. New York: Random House Publishing Group, 2007.

Hervieux, Sandy, Amanda Wheatley, Carey Toane, Lise Doucette, Paulina Rousseau, Michael Serafin, Michelle Spence, and Christina Kim. "The 99 AI Challenge: Empowering a University Community through an Open Learning Pilot." In *The Rise of AI: Implications and Applications of Artificial Intelligence in Academic Libraries*, edited by Sandy Hervieux and Amanda Wheatley, 3–14. Chicago: Association of College and Research Libraries, 2022.

Huang, K. "For Gen Z, TikTok Is the New Search Engine." *The New York Times*, September 17, 2022. www.nytimes.com/2022/09/16/technology/gen-z-tiktok-search-engine.html.

IBM Institute for Business Value. "Making Change Work . . . while the Work Keeps Changing." *Executive Report*. 2014. www.ibm.com/thought-leadership/institute-business-value/en-us/report/making-change-work.

IDEO. "IDEO U." www.ideou.com.

Kelley, T. *The Art of Innovation: Lessons in Creativity from IDEO, America's Leading Design Firm*. New York: Crown Publishers, 2007.

Koerber, Jennifer. "The Harvard Library: A Design Experiment in Library Futures." *Library Journal*, December 13, 2012. www.libraryjournal.com/story/the-harvard-library-a-design-experiment-in-library-futures.

Kohavi, Ronny, Thomas Crook, Roger Longbotham, Brian Frasca, Randy Henne, Juan Lavista Ferres, and Tamir Melamed. "Online Experimentation at Microsoft." Presentation at Microsoft ThinkWeek, 2009.

Lancaster, F. W., W. Lancaster, and M. J. Joncich. *The Measurement and Evaluation of Library Services*. Washington, DC: Information Resources Press, 1977.

Luca, M., and M. H. Bazerman. *The Power of Experiments: Decision-Making in a Data-Driven World*. Cambridge, MA: MIT Press, 2020.

Masters, Kiri. "Here's Everything That's Wrong with Amazon Spark." *Forbes*, May 20, 2018.

Mathews, Brian. "Think Like a Startup: A White Paper to Inspire Library Entrepreneurialism." *VTechWorks*, 2012.

Maxwell, John C. *Failing Forward: Turning Mistakes into Stepping Stones for Success*. Nashville, TN: Thomas Nelson Publishers, 2007.

Merchant, B. *The One Device: The Secret History of the iPhone*. Boston: Little, Brown and Company, 2017.

Michalko, M. *Thinkertoys: A Handbook of Creative-Thinking Techniques*. New York: Random House, 2010.

Morley, Bonnie. "Lists of Opportunities: My Experience as a School Librarian during the COVID-19 Pandemic." *Partnership: The Canadian Journal of Library and Information Practice and Research* 16, no. 1 (2021): 1–5.

Munro, K. *Tactical Urbanism for Librarians: Quick, Low-Cost Ways to Make Big Changes*. Chicago: ALA Editions, 2017.

Nuccilli, Maria, Elliot Polak, and Alex Binno. "Start with an Hour a Week: Enhancing Usability at Wayne State University Libraries." *Weave: Journal of Library User Experience* 1, no. 8 (2018).

Scott, Adam, and Dave Waddell. *The Experience Book: For Designers, Thinkers & Makers*. London: Black Dog Press, 2022.

Sinek, Simon. "Start with Why: How Great Leaders Inspire Action." Filmed September 16, 2009, in Seattle, WA. TED video, 18:34, www.ted.com/talks/simon_sinek_how_great_leaders_inspire_action/c.

Smith, Cynthia E. "Interview with Corinne Hill, Director, Chattanooga Public Library." In *By the People: Designing a Better America*, 214–21. New York: Cooper Hewitt, Smithsonian Design Museum, 2016.

Stephens, Rob. "Getting Started with TikTok for Library Marketing." *Public Services Quarterly* 18, no. 1 (2022): 59–64. DOI: 10.1080/15228959.2021.2008286.

Stuart, Crit et al. "An Experiment in Modern Knowledge Spaces: The Library East Commons." Video produced by Hugh Crawford's English 1102 class. Georgia Institute of Technology, 2006. hdl.handle.net/1853/13665. 2006.

Thomke, S. H. *Experimentation Works: The Surprising Power of Business Experiments*. Cambridge, MA: Harvard Business Review Press, 2020.

Thomke, Stefan. "Building a Culture of Experimentation." *Harvard Business Review* 98, no. 2 (March–April 2020): 40–48.

Vercelletto, Christina. "Welcoming the Curious." *Library Journal* 143, no. 16 (2018): 20–23.

Wayne State University Library System. "Library System Visionary Pillars." https://library.wayne.edu/info/about/visionary-pillars/.

Wright, Jason. "Georgia Tech Library Opens in Refurbished Crosland Tower." *Georgia Tech News Center*, January 11, 2019. https://news.gatech.edu/news/2019/01/11/georgia-tech-library-opens-refurbished-crosland-tower.

INDEX

#
2SLGBTQ+ resources, 83
3D scanning, 86–89, 97
3Doodler, 96, 108, 109, 110–111*f*
99 AI Challenge, 79–80

A
A/B testing, 16–17
administrators, 23, 126–127, 130, 136–140, 145–146, 149
AIGA, 73
Alford, Larry, 76–78
Amazon, experimentation by, 19, 123–124
ambassadors, 134, 145–146
Anderson, Laura, 76–81
Apple, as innovation leader, 3–4, 7, 38, 43, 157
approval process, 145–146, 147*f*
artificial intelligence (AI), xii, 53, 79–80
assessment phase of IDEEA, 63, 101–116, 134
augmented reality (AR), 58, 61, 154

B
baby boomers, as team members, 132
Ball, Melissa C., 90–91
behaviors, in lifecycle mapping, 46–47
beta spaces, 73–74. *See also* space-based experiments
Bezos, Jeff, 19, 124
bias, 17, 60, 105, 125–126
Booking.com, 127–128, 146, 148, 152
brainstorming, 41–42, 43–44, 51–53, 130–131
branch libraries, 64–65, 115
branding and rebranding, 97–99
budgets, limited, 137, 150–151

C
Carnegie Mellon University (CMU), 28–29
cataloging bias, 125–126
centralized teams, 155
ChatGPT, xii
Chattanooga Public Library, 73
close-ended questions, 104
collaborator-based teams, 141
committees, 66–67, 148–150, 155. *See also* teams
communication plans, 144, 145*f*, 152–153
companies. *See* technology companies
concept maps, 44–45*f*
conferences
    attending, 5–6, 43, 97, 131, 137
    presenting at, 97
control groups, 18, 62–63
coordinators, 148–150, 155
COVID-19, 81–84
creativity
    vs. innovation, 5–6
    uncertainty and, 22, 129–130
curiosity, power of, 3–11, 130

163

D

data assessment, 63, 101–116, 134
data collection
    bias in, 17, 60, 105
    considerations for, 59–64, 101–102, 122
    examples of, 35–36
    librarians' expertise in, 8, 9, 134
    tools for, 102–108
dataCoLAB, 29
decentralized teams, 155
decision-making, 4, 15, 17, 20, 23
design phase of IDEEA, 57–69, 122
design thinking, 42–44, 48–56, 156–157
Design Thinking for Libraries Toolkit (IDEO), 48–49, 56
designed experience, x
digitization experiments, 27–28, 154–155
displays, 72
diversity, equity, and inclusion, 44–45, 78–79, 93, 125–126, 149
documentation, post-experiment, 94–97
Dropbox, success of, 7–8

E

Eames, Charles and Ray, 126, 128
Einstein, Albert, 43
Electric Campfire experiment, 75, 76*f*
Ellender Library, 89, 90
empathy, as foundation of design thinking, 49, 51
employees
    generational differences in, 131–132
    job descriptions of, 134–136
    rewards and incentives for, 145*f*, 150–151
    See also librarians; teams
engage phase of IDEEA, 85–99
equity, diversity, and inclusion, 44–45, 78–79, 93, 125–126, 149
evaluation methods, 109–116
The Experience Book (Scott and Waddell), x
An Experiment in Modern Knowledge Spaces (Stuart et al.), 30
experiment phase of IDEEA, 71–84

experimentation
    administration and, 23, 126–127, 130, 136–140, 145–146, 149
    assessment phase of, 63, 101–116, 134
    barriers to, 4, 22–23, 94, 136, 138–139, 155–157
    building a culture of, 4–5, 7–11, 13–14, 18–24, 25–38, 145*f*
    curiosity and, 3–11, 130
    design phase of, 57–69, 122
    engage phase of, 85–99
    experiment phase of, 71–84
    ideation phase of, 41–56, 64, 72, 93
    roadmap for, 143–158
    role of play and discovery in, 10, 78, 98, 153
    small changes as, 14, 23–24, 32–34, 36
    by technology companies (*see* technology companies)
    tools for incentivizing, 145*f*, 150–151
    See also innovation
experiments
    case studies of, 28–34, 65–68, 73–83, 90–93
    choice of, 56
    creating excitement about, 99
    every aspect of libraries as, 25–26, 35–38
    field or real-world, 17
    intentional *vs.* incidental, 35–36
    natural *vs.* lab, 16–17
    as needing to solve a problem, 42–45
    pop-up, 73–74, 94
    program-based, 28–29, 78–80
    vs. prototypes, 14
    scientific, 18
    space-based, 17, 29–32, 35–36, 61, 64, 73–75, 82–83, 104
    successful *vs.* unsuccessful, 113–116, 119–128, 148, 153
    technology-based, 27–28, 32–34, 79–80, 106–107

F

Facebook, 90
Failing Forward (Maxwell), 120

failure
  embracing and learning from, 67–68, 119–128, 130, 146, 153
  evaluating for, 113–116
  vs. mistakes, 128
  of start-ups, 124–125
Florida International University, 90–93
focus groups, 46, 50, 105–106, 108, 110–112
fyp, on TikTok, 89

G

Gen X team members, 132
Gen Z
  as team members, 131
  TikTok as search engine for, 88
generative AI, xii, 53
genrefication, 82, 84n10
Georgia Tech Library, 29–32
"Getting Started with TikTok for Library Marketing" (Stephens), 89–90
goals, tangible, 140. *See also* objectives
Google
  focus on play and fun at, 10
  free innovation time at, 135
  number of experiments conducted by, 16
  vs. OpenAI, xii
Google Forms, 103, 104
Gothelf, Jeff, 33
government sector, 65–68
Graduate School of Design (Harvard), 74
Green Library at FIU, 90–93
green light, getting the, 145–146, 147*f*
growth mindset, need for, 5–6, 23

H

Hammill, Sarah J., 90–91
Harvard Business Review, 146
Harvard University, 17, 74–75
hashtags, 89, 108, 124
Heatherwick, Thomas, 21
hiring practices, 136

Houston, Drew, 7–8
"how might we?," asking, 43–44, 53–54
human-centered approach, 41, 45–50, 95, 156–157
hypotheses, 58–60, 69

I

IBM, on middle managers, 138
idea banks, 154
ideation phase, 41–56, 64, 72, 93
IDEEA process
  as anti-method, xi, 41–42
  assessment phase, 63, 101–116, 134
  design phase, 57–69, 122
  engage phase, 85–99
  experiment phase, 71–84
  ideation phase, 41–56, 64, 72, 93
IDEO, 48–49, 131
Implicit Association Test (IAT), 17
implicit bias, 17
incentives and rewards, 145*f*, 150–151
incidental experiments, 35–36
inclusion, equity, and diversity, 44–45, 78–79, 93, 125–126, 149
Indigo Adopt a School, 83
information professionals. *See* librarians
innovation
  vs. creativity, 5–6
  experimentation as precursor to, 9, 19, 23, 38
  experiments as tool to fuel, 9
  as a good idea executed well, 13, 42–43
  insight as foundation of, 49–50
  by technology companies and start-ups, 3–11
  See also experimentation
Innovation Awards at UTL, 75–81
insight, as foundation of design thinking, 49–50
Instagram, 88–89, 90, 108, 109, 112
intentional experiments, 35–36
interviews and focus groups, 46, 50, 105–106, 108, 110–112

intuition bias, 17, 139
iPad experiments, 96, 115, 120–121
iPhones, development of, 3–4, 7, 38, 43, 157

J
job descriptions, 134–136

K
key performance indicators (KPIs), 112

L
lab experiments *vs.* natural experiments, 16–17
Labrary, 73–74
leadership, skills for, 132–134, 137–141
Lean UX (Gothelf), 33
librarians
    curiosity in, 5–6, 9, 130
    data collection expertise of, 8, 9, 134
    repetitive work of, 22–23
    skills needed by, 129–141
    with user-experience expertise, 134
    See also employees
librarianship
    need for a growth mindset in, 5–6, 23
    as slower moving discipline, 4, 5
libraries
    barriers to experimentation in, 4, 22–23, 94, 136, 138–139, 155–157
    branch and satellite, 64–65, 115
    branding and rebranding of, 97–99
    building a culture of experimentation in, 4–5, 7–11, 13–14, 18–24, 25–38
    case studies of, 28–34, 73–83, 90–93
    displays as attractions in, 72
    as every aspect being an experiment, 25–26, 35–38
    on Instagram, 88–89
    satisfying experiences at, 21
    in schools during the pandemic, 81–83
    spaces and layouts in, 17, 29–32, 35–36, 61, 64, 73–75, 82–83, 104
    vs. technology companies, 8, 19–21, 25–26, 143

Library East Commons (LEC) at Georgia Tech, 29–32
Library Journal, 97
Library of Congress classification system, 125–126
Library Test Kitchen, 74–75
lifecycle mapping, 46–47*f*
Lin, Geraldine, 97–98
LinkedIn Learning, 110, 131
Lists of Opportunities (Morley), 81
Looking Glass, 91, 96, 121, 122
Los Angeles (LA) County Library, 97–98
Luca, Michael, 35

M
"Making Room for Innovation" (Goldenson and Hill), 73–74
managers and administrators, 23, 126–127, 130, 136–140, 145–146, 149
maps
    concept maps, 44–45*f*
    lifecycle maps, 46–47*f*
marketing, 88–93, 97–99
Massachusetts Institute of Technology Libraries, 136
Mathews, Brian, 28–29, 31*f,* 32, 138
Maxwell, John C., 120
The Measurement and Evaluation of Library Services (Lancaster et al.), 101
Media Memory experiment, 75
"'Meet, Greet, and Eat' Outreach" (Ball et al.), 90–91
mentoring programs, 134
Microsoft, failure at, 123
middle managers, 23, 138
millennial team members, 131–132
mistakes *vs.* failures, 128
models, as prototypes, 14–15
mood boards, 55
Morley, Bonnie, 81–83

N
natural experiments *vs.* lab experiments, 16–17

The New York Times, 88
news article exercise, 54–55*f*

O

objectives, 59, 62–64, 66, 112–113, 115, 122, 128, 148
observation
    as data collection tool, 104–105, 110, 111*f*
    as foundation of design thinking, 49, 50–51
    grid for, 110, 111*f*
open houses and playdays, 90–93
Open Science & Data Collaborations (OSDC), 28–29
OpenAI, xii
open-ended questions, 53–54, 110–112
outreach and engagement, 85–99

P

pandemic, momentum from, 81–84
partnerships, 93–94
patrons. *See* users
PGH Lab, 65–68
pilot testing. *See* prototyping and testing
pink zones, 145*f,* 154
Pittsburgh's PGH Lab initiative, 65–68
play and discovery, fostering, 10, 78, 98, 153
playdays and open houses, 90–93
Polak, Elliot, 32–33, 34
pop-up experiments, 73–74, 94
The Power of Experiments (Luca and Bazerman), 35
problems, identifying, 42–45, 52
program-based experiments, 28–29, 78–80
project-based teams, 141
prototyping and testing, 4, 13–24, 38, 57–58, 61–62, 69, 103*f,* 151

Q

QR code example, 58, 61
qualitative *vs.* quantitative research, 105–112

questionnaires and surveys, 46, 102–104, 108, 110
questions
    close-ended, 104
    "how might we?," 43–44, 53–54
    open-ended, 53–54, 110–112
    "why not?," 10

R

Rausch, Daniel, 124
rebranding, 97–99
recipes, at Library Test Kitchen, 75
research and design (R&D), investment in, 19–21
research bias, 17, 60, 105
research questions. *See* hypotheses
rewards and incentives, 145*f,* 150–151
The Rise of AI (Hervieux and Wheatley), 79
Rovio, 125

S

scanning, 3D, 86–89, 97
school libraries, 81–83
scientific experiments, 18
Sense Scanners, 86–87, 91
service sector *vs.* technology sector, 19–21
Sinek, Simon, 43
skills, essential, 129–141
Skip the Scan, 82, 83
social media, 88–90, 107–108, 112, 123–124
Sorondo, Barbara M., 90–91
South by Southwest (SXSW), 10, 97
space-based experiments, 17, 29–32, 35–36, 61, 64, 73–75, 82–83, 104
Spark, failure of, 123–124
"Start with an Hour a Week" (Nuccilli et al.), 33
"Start with Why" (Sinek), 43
start-ups
    Dropbox as successful example of, 7–8
    as epitome of experimentation, 7–8, 25
    failure rate of, 124–125
    focus on play and fun at, 10
    at PGH Lab, 65–68
    See also technology companies

status quo
  bias towards, 17
  challenges to, 72, 84, 138, 139, 156
  as control group, 18, 62–63
Stephens, Rob, 89–90
Stoll, Trevor, 65–68
storytelling, 95, 108
subject headings, bias in, 125–126
submission process, 77, 144, 145f, 146, 147f, 148
success
  evaluating experiments for, 113–116
  failure as a tool for, 120–121, 126
  of organizational teams, 140–141
  skills needed for, 130–132
surveys, 102–104, 108, 110

T

Tableau, 110
taglines, 98
teams
  being a leader of, 133–134, 138–139
  brainstorming by, 43–44
  diversification of, 136
  organization of, 141, 144–145f, 153–155
  skills of members in, 131–132
  tips for success with, 140–141
  See also committees; employees
TechCrunch, xii
technology companies
  as constant experimenters, 4, 16, 19–20
  curiosity and creativity in, 3–11
  failures by, 123–125, 127–128
  focus on play and fun at, 10
  vs. libraries, 8, 19–21, 25–26, 143
  as start-ups (*see* start-ups)
  testing and prototyping by, xii, 3, 15–16, 19–21, 38
  See also specific companies
technology sector *vs.* service sector, 19–21
technology-based experiments, 27–28, 32–34, 79–80, 106–107
testing and prototyping, 3–4, 13–24, 38, 57–58, 61–62, 69, 103f, 151

Think Like a Startup (Mathews), 138
Thinkertoys (Michalko), 56
TikTok, 88, 89–90

U

uncertainty, 7, 22, 129–130, 139
University Chief Librarian's Innovation Awards, 75–81
University of Toronto Libraries (UTL), 75–81
University of Toronto UX concentration, 134
usability tests, 33, 106–107, 112
user experience (UX), 33, 57, 102–107, 109, 112, 113, 134
user-centered hypotheses, 58–59
users
  empathy for, 49, 51
  engaging with, 85–91
  feedback from, 45–46, 102–106, 108, 110–112
  hypotheses focused on, 58–59
  lifecycle mapping the behaviors of, 46–47
  observation of, 49, 50–51
  sharing results with, 94–97

V

values, shared, 145f, 152–153
variables, in experiment types, 16, 18
Vercelletto, Christina, 97–98
"Visionary Pillars" model, 34

W

Wayne State University (WSU) Libraries, 32–34, 36, 60, 64
web analytics, 106–107, 112
web design experiments, 32–34, 64
"Welcoming the Curious" (Vercelletto), 97–98
"why not?," asking, 10

You may also be interested in...

ISBN: 978-0-8389-1226-3

ISBN: 978-0-8389-3958-1

ISBN: 978-0-8389-3840-9

ISBN: 978-0-8389-3785-3

For more titles, visit **alastore.ala.org**